ANATOMY
OF THE CHINESE
BUSINESS MIND

An Insider's Perspective

ANATOMY
OF THE CHINESE
BUSINESS MIND

An Insider's Perspective

Fangyuan Yuan   Meiru Liu

CENGAGE
Learning™

Australia • Brazil • Japan • Korea • Mexico • Singapore • Spain • United Kingdom • United States

Anatomy of the Chinese Business Mind
Fangyuan Yuan, Meiru Liu

Publishing Director:
Paul Tan

Senior Development Editor:
Liping Yang

Assistant Publishing Manager:
Pauline Lim

Production Executive:
Cindy Chai

Senior Product Director:
Janet Lim

Product Managers:
Kevin Joo
Lee Hong Tan

Copy Editor:
Rosemary Lim

Illustrator:
Ng Huk Keng

Cover Designer:
Melvin Chong

Compositor:
Gantec Solutions

ISBN-13: 978-981-4239-17-2
ISBN-10: 981-4239-17-8

Cengage Learning Asia Pte Ltd
5 Shenton Way #01-01
UIC Building
Singapore 068808

Cengage Learning is a leading provider of customized learning solutions with office locations around the globe, including Singapore, the United Kingdom, Australia, Mexico, Brazil, and Japan. Locate your local office at:
www.cengage.com/global

Cengage Learning products are represented in Canada by Nelson Education, Ltd.

For product information, visit **www.cengageasia.com**

Printed in Singapore
2 3 4 5 6 7 13 12 11 10

Table of Contents

Preface

FROM OUTSIDE TO INSIDE

Every semester on the first day of our Chinese language class, we always ask our students why they have decided to learn Chinese, a language that needs four times longer to master than Spanish or French. We're not surprised when nine out of ten say they're learning Chinese because they plan to go to China. Some even say that if they don't know how to communicate in Chinese they will be at a competitive disadvantage since the 21st century belongs to China. Their answers seem to be a perfect footnote to what M. Jean-Luc Chéreau, the president of Carrefour China, said in an interview: "Everybody is dreaming about China" (Child 2006).

However, when we ask our students what they know about China their answers vary: "China is very big." "China has the largest population in the world." "China has a long history." "Chinese food is delicious." "Stuff made in China is good and cheap." "Chinese *gongfu* (martial arts) is amazing." "China is still a developing country but is developing amazingly fast." "America has outsourced a lot of jobs to China." "There are a lot of opportunities in China."

Looking at these young faces full of hope for the future, we don't know if they can fully understand the following remark on China by Chéreau: "We are in another world. If you come to China with preconceived ideas after having been successful in Europe or the United States, you make mistake after mistake" (Child 2006). Our students live far from China but are hoping to gain inside information through learning its language, whereas Chéreau has lived and worked in China for more than ten years. What does Chéreau mean by "different world" and "mistake after mistake"?

Carrefour is the second largest retailer in the world (after Wal-Mart) and the largest, most successful foreign retailer in China. Chéreau uses his ten years of experience with Carrefour in China to back up his comments, setting himself somewhere between being an insider and an outsider in China. As authors of this book we are also guiding readers in an attempt to shift from outsider to insider through similar stories on how to do business in China.

WHO ARE WE?

We are both China-born, China-raised, and China-educated to college and graduate level. In the 1980s and 1990s, we came to the United States for our doctoral degrees, having already spent some time teaching in Chinese universities, working as organizers of international trade shows in China, translators for English-speaking Western visitors to China, and having attended international conferences in China and other countries. We had opportunities to experience and learn about the differences between what we had been taught about foreigners and what foreign visitors were actually doing. We rarely thought about why people from different cultures approached things in different ways. When we first arrived in the United States as students, we experienced every aspect of culture shock, from the relatively simple dishes with which Americans entertained their guests at home to the ways in which a term paper should be structured and developed. We were surprised that a ten-year-old boy addressed his stepfather by his first name and felt shocked that a talk-show anchor could joke about the president of the nation. We began to explore the reason why.

Now both of us are teaching Chinese language and culture at American universities. In addition, we are invited to give lectures, work as consultants to government agencies, institutions, and multinational corporations, and conduct cross-cultural workshops and seminars on topics ranging from etiquette at Chinese banquets to the macro-economic situation after China was admitted to the World Trade Organization. Our students and trainees include college students, MBA students, managers, engineers, CEOs, as well as government officials. They are eager to learn about China, the country in which they plan to start business, develop a career, or from where they have recently returned with a view to visiting again. Our profession has enabled us to closely examine the Chinese culture of our upbringing and also the American culture of our students and trainees.

Regarded as "experts" and "insiders" of the Chinese business world, we often meet baffled business people recently returned from a trade trip in China, some of whom are our students and trainees. They come to us seeking answers as to why they have failed in business when they had hoped to gain. Some even want to find out if their Chinese business counterparts' elusive response means "yes" or "no." Seeing our students' great interest and talking with those who have experienced cultural bungles, we feel the need to extend our discussion to more people. This is the inspiration for writing this book on Chinese culture in general and Chinese business culture in particular.

How This Book Differs?

There are several books in the market about doing business in China. They are well researched and accurate in their descriptions of how the Chinese conduct business. However, most of these are authored by Western scholars and very few are written from an insider's perspective. This book has the following distinct advantages over other similar books on the market:

- Our insider's perspective stands us in good stead to tell our readers not only how Chinese people act on certain occasions but also how they expect foreigners to act, letting you know why you should do something in a certain way;
- Using simple language and humorous illustrations we have created a guide book that is easy to follow with abundant tips, cultural insights, and useful information for business people planning a trip to China;
- While elucidating how Chinese people do business, we trace the roots of present-day Chinese business culture in China's past, presenting an overview of Chinese culture, history, philosophy, people, and special characteristics;
- Our years of teaching and lecturing in the US have allowed us to collect case studies which we use to illustrate theoretical analysis and factual explanations, providing a more vivid and concrete picture of the cultural hurdles that foreigners often come across when living and doing business in China.

WHAT'S INSIDE?

This book can be divided into three parts, although with some overlapping. The first part, Chapters 1 and 2, give readers a general overview of China, including its history, geography, people, language, the economic reforms over the past 30 years, business environment, socio-economic conditions, and possible challenges and opportunities for foreign businesses. Through these two chapters, readers can obtain a macro picture of what has shaped China today. This helps establish a basis for exploring the "Chinese Business Mind." Chapters 3 through 6 make up the second part in which we focus more on the historical, philosophical, and cultural underpinnings that have influenced the people of China in their general outlooks on the world, behavior patterns, and the way to conduct business with foreigners. In Part Two, we introduce three iconic figures in Chinese culture and their philosophies, China's traditional business culture, and regional business culture.

The remaining nine chapters make up the third part, which focuses on how foreigners should conduct themselves while living and working in China. We summarize *guanxi* and face, two most important notions that underlie the way business is conducted in China, how our readers may be received and viewed as a foreigner, what you may experience at the negotiation table, in addition to the customs and etiquette generally followed in the Chinese business world.

The appendices contain more information for the convenience of our readers. They include a timeline of Chinese history, major historical events since 1949, a list of Chinese holidays, names of provinces, regions, and municipalities, the hierarchical government structure, types of foreign investment, typical dishes from different parts of China, and some basic survival phrases and sentences in Chinese.

WHO IS THIS BOOK FOR?

This book is written for readers who plan to go to China for business, expatriates living and working in China, students preparing to develop a career in China, and anyone interested in the topic. Tourists to China will also find much of the information practical and useful when planning their trip or during their stay in the country.

Acknowledgments

We are deeply indebted to our editor, Mr. Yang Liping, for his constant support, guidance, and suggestions on the content and format of the book. Without his help and patience, this project would not have been possible. Our special thanks also go to Mr. Arthur Sun who helped shape the project in the initial stages and provided valuable support throughout the process. We are greatly indebted to Ms. Yan Zhang, Professor of Chinese at Wyoming University, for her insights on China's traditional and regional business culture. We acknowledge our colleagues and students at the University of Pennsylvania, Portland State University, and the US Naval Academy.

Lastly, our sincerest thanks go to our families both in China and America for their love, care, support, and patience over the years.

Part One

A Bird's Eye View of China

1 China at a Glance

A s part of your preparation for a visit to China, it's important for you to read about the country, its history, culture, people, climate, religions, and so on. The reasons for this are many, but in this chapter we concentrate on just one: a knowledge of China will help you find some common ground with your Chinese partners, something that will be of tremendous benefit to your business. The reason is simple: Chinese people are very proud of their 5,000-year history and love to work with people who show interest in their culture. This chapter, therefore, provides an introductory sketch of China, offering insights, observations, and suggestions. If this short chapter inspires you to learn more about China and its culture then you'll find many in-depth books available in bookshops.

HISTORY

Imperial China

China is one of the world's oldest continuous civilizations with a history of about 5,000 years. Its beginnings date back to the legendary Xia Dynasty, around 2,000 BC, although the country was first unified under the name of a large empire in 221 BC when the Qin Dynasty (221 BC–206 BC) began. Unification was realized under the reign of China's first emperor Qin Shihuang (259 BC–210 BC) after many turbulent years of wars among different states. Qin Shihuang is a controversial figure in history. During his reign he adopted a legalist form of government, and brutally silenced other schools of thought, which included the burning of books and burying alive about 400 Confucian scholars. However, Qin Shihuang's contributions to the unification of the country cannot be ignored. He standardized written Chinese, the country's currency, and a system of measurement. He expanded roads and canals and started to build the famous Great Wall. Most important of all, perhaps, his administrative structure of centralized bureaucracy became the model for ruling the country for the next 2,000 years. Historians consider the Qin Dynasty as the beginning of Imperial China, a period which lasted about 2,000 years and came to the end with the collapse of the Qing Dynasty (1644–1912) in 1911.

The name of "China" in the Chinese language means "Middle Kingdom" (中国 *Zhongguo*) or the center of the universe. This Middle Kingdom was occupied by the relatively homogeneous Han Chinese, the largest ethnic group in the world today. The name *Han* comes from the Han Dynasty (206 BC–AD 220) that came after the Qin. Arts and culture flourished during the Han Dynasty, making it one of the greatest periods in Chinese history. It was during this period that Confucianism was first adopted as the state ideology and the Confucian ideal became a reference point and moral standard for both the ruler and the ruled. During the 2,000-year-long imperial era, China underwent numerous wars, witnessed the rise and fall of successive dynasties, and experienced periods of unification and fragmentation. However, its distinctive culture, which was deeply rooted in Confucianism, remained intact. Even in the periods when the country was ruled by non-Han ethnic groups, such as the Mongols and Manchus, the non-Han rulers were gradually assimilated into the Han culture.

For most of its long history, China implemented an isolationist, closed-door policy that came to an end when the British forcibly opened the country to foreign trade during the First Opium War (1839–1842). The British wanted to buy silk and tea from China, but being self-sufficient, China had little or no interest in British products. In order to trade with China, the British began trafficking opium, despite the fact that the drug was forbidden by the Chinese government. The large amounts of opium being trafficked by the British resulted in many Chinese becoming addicts and an outflow of a large amount of Chinese money. In 1839, the Qing government announced the abolition of the opium trade and a high-ranking official, Lin Zexu (1785–1850), confiscated hundreds of pounds of opium that were later burned in public. Upon the announcement of closing Canton Port, the only port in China opened to foreign trade, the British launched a war and defeated the Chinese with their modern artillery. In 1842, the Qing government was forced to sign an unequal treaty in which Hong Kong was ceded to Britain and China had to open more ports for foreign trade. The terms of this treaty were not fully carried out by either side and, in 1856, the Second Opium War broke out. China was defeated again and forced to grant more privileges to the British and other Western powers.

Defeat in the Opium Wars shattered China's Middle Kingdom mentality and greatly weakened the Qing's rule. By the second half of the 19th century, China plunged into social chaos, compounded by floods, famine, and government corruption. The country witnessed several rebellions, including the anti-foreign Taiping Rebellion (1850) and The Boxer Uprising (1900), as well as internal governmental political reforms. In 1911, a revolutionary uprising led by Sun Yat Sen (1866–1925), a republican and anti-Qing activist, toppled the Qing Dynasty, ending the millennia-old dynastic system of Imperial China.

FYI

Most Chinese are proud of their 5,000-year history. From time to time, you may sense a certain level of cultural superiority and pride from your Chinese friends and business partners. This may make you feel uncomfortable. At the same time, you may find that a lot of young Chinese admire almost everything from the West. They know more about Western culture, history, and ideologies than most educated Westerners would know about similar subjects in China. They learn English, celebrate Western holidays, such as Christmas and Valentine's Day, and imitate Western lifestyles. Such contradictory phenomena of national pride and admiration of the West may make you feel perplexed. Hopefully this short introduction on the beginning and end of the imperial era in China will help you better understand the reasons for this dichotomy.

The Republic of China

Sun Yat Sen was inaugurated as the Provisional President of the Republic of China in Wuhan on January 1, 1912. The Kuomintang (Nationalist Party or KMT) was founded in the same year by his associate. However, these revolutionists did not have their own army to unify the country. This meant that for the first few decades of the 20th century China was fragmented and ruled over by competing warlords more concerned about their own political powers than national interests when faced with foreign threats. The Beiyang government in Beijing (1912–1928), the internationally recognized regime of the time, made several concessions to foreign powers in order to gain external support against its domestic rivals. At this time of political upheaval and foreign invasion, a number of intellectuals began to question China's millennia-old Confucianism-based tradition and look for ways to strengthen China by introducing Western ideologies and promoting vernacular Chinese versus classical Chinese. On May 4, 1919, the famous May Fourth Movement began when a student demonstration broke out in Beijing against the Versailles Treaty that asked China to grant Shandong to Japan. This movement soon gained nationwide momentum and spread to other parts of the country, eventually leading to the founding of the Chinese Communist Party (CCP) in 1921 by some leftist intellectuals who had lost faith in Western-style liberal democracy.

Sun died of cancer in 1925 and the leadership of the KMT was taken over by Chiang Kai Shek (1887–1975), another important historical figure in modern Chinese history. Eventually the internal strife and factions grew into a civil war between the Communists and the KMT. In 1927, the KMT launched a massacre of the CCP. Among those who managed to escape was a young Communist named Mao Zedong, who later became one of the most important figures in the history of modern China. In 1934, the KMT routed the Communists, forcing them to flee to the hinterlands in an event known as the Long March. Mao consolidated his position during the Long March as the primary CCP leader.

In 1931, the Japanese seized Manchuria—the current three provinces of Heilongjiang, Jilin, and Liaoning in Northeast China—and in 1937 started the Sino–Japanese War. This led to a three-way fight in which the KMT, Communists, and Japanese battled for control of the country. None of the parties was able to gain the upper hand, although the KMT and the Communists did form an alliance against the Japanese. After Japan's defeat in 1945, the Communists and KMT returned to open civil war. This ended in 1949 when two million KMT supporters fled to Taiwan. On October 1,

1949, Mao Zedong proclaimed the founding of the People's Republic of China (PRC) with Beijing as capital.

FYI

The Chinese Communist Party considers three groups of members as the Party elite: those who participated in the Long March; those who participated in the Anti-Japanese War; and those who participated in the Civil War against the KMT. The first generation of PRC leaders belonged to the first group, including Mao Zedong and Deng Xiaoping, but few are alive today. The communist veterans of these groups enjoy special privileges as heroes of the nation. Nowadays, most of these veterans have passed away but their families' second or even third generations have begun to enter the political arena and take up important positions in local and central governments. Many of them are well educated and some have received education in Western countries.

The People's Republic of China

Immediately after the PRC was founded by the Chinese Communist Party in 1949, the new government set about countering the effects of centuries of economic mismanagement and 40 years of armed conflict. By 1952, despite participating in the Korean War (1950–1953), the Chinese government had brought industrial production back to the levels prior to the Sino–Japanese War, controlled inflation, and instituted land and political reforms. In 1953, the government inaugurated the first of its series of Five-Year Plans, a Soviet economic practice planned to augment agricultural and industrial output by designating quotas for every five-year period. Following the Soviet model of central planning, the Chinese government set up a development plan for heavy industry and the collectivization of agricultural production. In 1958, with the goal of speeding up development, the government launched the Great Leap Forward by mobilizing the peasant masses to increase crop production and use excess labor to produce steel on a large scale. This resulted in a great famine, officially blamed on a natural disaster. At the beginning of the 1960s, the Chinese government broke with the Soviets and began to move away from the earlier heavy-industry production plan to focus on developing light industry and the agricultural sector.

In 1966, Mao launched the Great Cultural Revolution—actually the result of power struggles within the party. Mao called upon college and high school students, the so-called "Red Guards," to rebel against every sphere of authority. This mass movement resulted in the deaths of many state leaders and well-known scholars, including China's president Liu Shaoqi. China collapsed into chaos with schools shut down, offices closed, and transportation disrupted. Fighting, bloodshed, and destruction were everywhere. This chaotic situation came to an end with Mao's death in 1976.

In 1971, China was recognized by the United Nations and began to develop relationships with non-communist countries, most importantly the United States. It was a sign that China was coming out of its old isolationist shell to achieve its legitimate place in the international community. In 1978, Deng Xiaoping launched the Four Modernizations Drive: the economic reforms of agriculture, industry, science and technology, and national defense. He initiated the Open Door Policy in 1979, through which China began to look beyond its borders for help in developing its economy. More detailed information about this economic reform is provided in the next chapter.

FYI

Although living standards were incredibly low during the Mao era, many low-income people today still cherish those days when everybody was equal in almost every aspect: income, housing, and benefits. City residents did not have to spend money to go to school and see a doctor. They were assigned a job upon graduation and allocated a dwelling place at a symbolic rent of a few dimes. If you take a taxi in China, you may find an image of Mao Zedong hung in the car. The driver may complain to you about how unfair society is today. He may tell you that his wife has been laid off, they cannot afford to buy a decent apartment, or he has to pay his son's college tuition, which is about two years of his income. For such taxi drivers, Mao Zedong is worshipped as if he were a god to protect the poor.

POPULATION

With a population of more than 1.3 billion, about one-fourth of the world's total, China is the world's most populous country. The population is distributed unevenly with densely populated coastal areas in the east and sparsely populated inland areas in the west. To slow down its rapid population growth, China enforced a one-child family planning policy at the end of the 1970s. Although the one-child policy has effectively reduced the population growth rate, it has made the country one of the most rapidly aging countries in the world. The side effects of this policy include a shortage of labor in the near future and a heavy social burden for taking care of the aged. However, the Chinese government has recently stated that the one-child policy will remain effective for at least the next decade. In reality some exceptions can be granted, say, to couples to have more than one child if both of them are the only child in their families.

FYI

You may have some reservations about the one-child policy, but if you have a chance to work and live in the world's most populous country you may change your mind. Imagine that wherever you go you will always find crowds of people: bus stations, trains, shopping centers, restaurants, and beauty spots. In no time you'll feel like escaping. Because of China's large population, the Chinese have a much stronger sense of competition. Don't be surprised when you come across an advertisement for an English learning program targeting kindergarteners as illustrated below.

Competition begins as a baby

Some serious social problems have occurred as a result of the one-child policy. For example, China does not have a well-established social security system and, according to tradition, children have an obligation to take care of their aging parents. Under the one-child policy, young people have to take care of a lot more elders than previous generations. Another issue is that people born after the enforcement of this policy may have no brothers or sisters and their children may have no aunts, uncles, and cousins. This means that within a few decades, the traditional kinship system may no longer exist.

GEOGRAPHY

China has an area of 9.6 million square kilometers, almost as large as Europe and about one-fifteenth of the world's land mass. It is the third largest country in the world, next to Canada and Russia. Situated in East Asia, China is bounded by the Pacific in the east and bordered by Mongolia, India, Pakistan, Nepal, Bhutan, Myanmar, Laos, Vietnam, North Korea, Russia, Tajikistan, Kyrgyzstan, Kazakhstan, and Afghanistan in the north, south, and west.

China's location on the world map

Administrative Divisions

For administrative purposes, China is divided into 23 provinces (for example, Jiangsu, Anhui), five autonomous regions (for example, Tibet, Inner Mongolia), four central administrative municipalities (Beijing, Shanghai, Tianjin, and Chongqing), and two special administrative regions (known as SAR: Hong Kong and Macau). Municipalities are under the direct administration of the central government.

Map of China and her administrative divisions

Time Zone

Though vast in size, China has only one time: Beijing time is the standard time throughout the country. Beijing is located at E8 time zone, eight

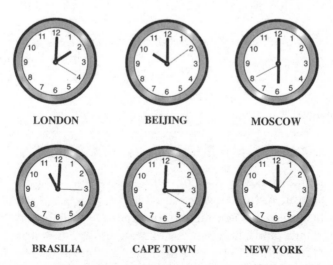

Time zones of China and other countries

hours earlier than the Greenwich Mean Time (GMT). So be careful if you want to call somebody in Xinjiang at 9:00 in the morning. They may still be asleep while people in Beijing and Shanghai have already started to work.

Climate

China's climate is extremely diverse due to its vast size. It is tropical in the south and almost sub-arctic in the north. The northern part of Heilongjiang, in northeastern China, has almost no summer, while Hainan Island in southern China has a long summer with no winter. The Huaihe River valley features four distinct seasons; the western part of the Qinghai-Tibet Plateau is covered by snow all year round; the southern part of the Yunnan-Guizhou Plateau is spring-like all year; and the northwestern inland region sees a great temperature drop through one day. So if you travel to China, you need to pay close attention to the local weather.

PEOPLES

There are 56 ethnic groups in China. The Han people are the largest group, about 1.1 billion or 93.3% of the country's population. The other ethnic groups, or minority nationalities, make up about 160 million, including Mongolian, Miao, Hui, and Tibetan, to name a few. Generally speaking, the minority-inhabited areas are less developed than the Han areas.

China is so large that regional people differ in many respects. Identifying where someone comes from is important. A common question usually asked by one Chinese of another Chinese is "Where are you from?" A later chapter details regional differences. As a foreigner in China you will also be asked where you come from on first meeting someone.

FYI

Most people from Hong Kong, Macau, and Taiwan are more likely to identify themselves as the people of the region rather than Chinese. Such identification is particularly sensitive for people from Taiwan.

RELIGIONS

The religious traditions of China are Confucianism, Daoism, and Buddhism. However, unlike the institutionalized belief systems in the West, they are more like philosophies of life that influence the behaviors and beliefs of individuals and the functions of the state. This is especially the case with Confucianism. Other important religions in the country include Islam and Christianity. The Han Chinese are known as non-religious as a whole and few claim to be Buddhist or Daoist alone.

FYI

After the PRC was founded in 1949, and before the economic reforms in the late 1970s, people in China were not encouraged to practice any religions. Instead they were to follow communist ideology. During the Cultural Revolution, temples and churches were destroyed or closed as a sign that communism was the only ideology that people should follow. Nowadays, with a much more liberal political atmosphere, more and more people are beginning to practice religions of various kinds.

LANGUAGE

The Chinese language is the language of the Han people, the major ethnic group of China. About 1.3 billion people, or one-fifth of the world's population, speak one form of the language in the world. In China, approximately 95% of the population speaks the language, as opposed to non-Chinese languages, such as Tibetan, Mongolian, Lolo, Miao, and Tai. Besides Mainland China, Taiwan, and Hong Kong, Chinese is also spoken by a large population in Southeast Asia, especially in Singapore, Malaysia, Indonesia, and Thailand. Chinese-speaking communities can also be found in many parts of the world.

FYI

Chinese is one of the most difficult languages to master due to its tonal system and large number of characters. It is said that one needs four times longer to learn the language than learning Spanish or French. Don't feel intimidated. Common greetings and farewells are not difficult. A simple accented *"Ni Hao"* ("How are you?") will bring a smile to the face of your Chinese partners or clients. In Appendix I, we have collected a list of commonly used Chinese sentences for you to learn, imitate, and use.

The identification of the varieties of Chinese as languages or dialects is controversial. As a language family, the Mandarin language group is the largest with 850 million speakers, outnumbering any other language in the world. It is followed by Wu, 90 million speakers, and Cantonese, 80 million speakers. Cantonese is spoken in Guangdong, Hong Kong, and Macau, as well as in many overseas Chinese communities.

The Mandarin group alone consists of a wide range of dialects in the northern, central, and western regions. Its standardized form is called Standard Mandarin, known in China as *Putonghua*, the common language. It is called *Guoyu* (the national language) in Taiwan and *Huayu* (the Chinese language) in Singapore. Mandarin is the official language of the People's Republic of China and Taiwan, as well as one of the four official languages in Singapore and one of the six official languages of the United Nations. All forms of spoken Chinese are tonal with four tones in Mandarin and nine tones in Cantonese. Pinyin is the most commonly used romanized form of Standard Mandarin, introduced in 1956 by the People's Republic of China.

FYI

You should be aware that people who speak different Chinese dialects may often not be able to understand each other. Even people of the Mandarin group may have difficulty communicating with each other. However, educated people across the country can communicate in Standard Mandarin, even though local dialects are still spoken among the people from the same area.

In contrast to the great variety of spoken Chinese, written Chinese is the same across different dialects. There are two systems for written Chinese: the traditional and the simplified. The former, dating back to the late

Han dynasty, is used in Hong Kong, Taiwan, and Macau. The latter was developed by the PRC in 1956 to promote mass literacy through reduced character strokes. It is believed that a well-educated Chinese can recognize approximately 6,000 to 7,000 characters, but one can read newspapers with 3,000 characters.

FYI

You may sometimes find it difficult to grasp the gist of what your Chinese partner has said, even though you understand perfectly the surface meaning. You may also find that your Chinese friends use some form of evidence to support an argument that is not convincing to you at all. One reason is that the Chinese like to speak in a circular way rather than directly and use a lot of allusions and anecdotes that appear foreign to you but are an essential part of their culture. It is therefore important to find a qualified interpreter who can not only translate the literal meaning but also the connotations hidden behind the words.

Chapter 2

The Chinese Economy—Challenges and Opportunities

While Chapter 1 gave you an overall picture of China, in this chapter we begin to deal with specifics, providing an introduction to the past 30 years of China's economic development from a planned economy to a market-oriented economy. We focus on the reform of state-owned enterprises and the open-door policy, its impact on foreign trade and investment, social problems as by-products of the reform, and restrictions and options for foreign investors. Using case studies, observations, and suggestions, you will learn about possible challenges and opportunities, and ways to achieve your business goals when operating and investing in China.

A GLANCE AT THE REFORM

Achievements of the Reform

As briefly mentioned in Chapter 1, China launched its open-door policy and economic reforms in 1978 under the leadership of Deng Xiaoping. In the 30 years since, the world has witnessed rapid economic growth in China, including an average 9% increase in GDP, a jump to becoming the fourth largest economy, as well as an impressive increase in international trade and foreign direct investment. In addition, China now has a relatively stable investment environment, a large foreign exchange reserve, improved living standards, large numbers of private and foreign companies, more transparent administrative processes, and reformed fiscal, legal, and banking systems. Figure 2.1 and Table 2.1 provide a summary of these 30 years of reform and growth.

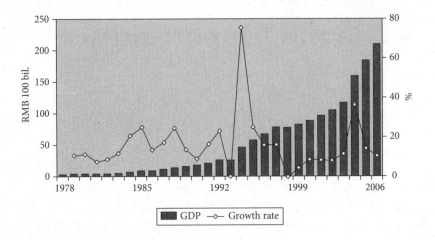

Figure 2.1 China's GDP growth: 1978–2006

Source: Center for China Studies, National Chengchi University, *China Economic Databases* (http://ics.nccu.edu.tw/eced/chinese/stats.html)

Table 2.1 China's GDP: Real growth rate from 2003–2008

Year	GDP: Real growth rate	Rank	Percentage change	Date of information
2003	8.00 %	11	—	2002 est.
2004	9.10 %	12	13.75 %	2003 est.
2005	9.10 %	17	0.00 %	2004 est.
2006	10.20 %	4*	12.09 %	2005 est.
2007	10.70 %	4**	4.90 %	2006 est.
2008	8.00 %***	—	—	2008 est.

Source: CIA (Central Intelligence Agency) World Factbook
Note: Using an annual growth rate of 8%, China's GDP in 2020 will be RMB 67 trillion.
*Listed by the IMF and the World Bank; **Listed by the *CIA World Factbook*.
*** Chinese Premier Wen Jiabao's government work report delivered at the opening meeting of the First Session of the 11th National People's Congress (NPC), the top legislature, on March 5, 2008.

Before the Reform

During the decades of controlled or command economy prior to 1978, China resembled a gigantic corporation (the so-called "China Incorporated") managed by the central government planners functioning as a board of directors (Shirk 1993, 25). For the first few years after the founding of the People's Republic of China in 1949, the government nationalized almost the entire industrial economy by taking over previously state-owned enterprises, subsidiaries of foreign firms, and a large number of private companies. This meant there were almost no private and foreign firms, only state-owned and collectively owned companies. Following the Soviet model, the state prioritized development in the heavy industry sector, but generally ignored light industry, agriculture, and service industries. The government directed and controlled a dominant share of economic output, setting production goals, regulating prices, and allocating limited resources. On an international level, China adopted a closed-door policy with very limited foreign trade under the strict control of the central government.

Beginning of Special Economic Zones: The Pearl River Delta

In 1978, with the aim of saving the national economy from collapse after 30 years of command economy, Deng Xiaoping launched an open-door policy and initiated internal economic reforms. The reforms started in the two southern provinces of Guangdong and Fujian, where the first four Special Economic Zones (SEZs) were established in the Pearl River Delta. The SEZs then expanded to 14 coastal cities and Hainan Island in southern China. Once part of Guangdong Province, Hainan became a separate province in 1988. It is now the largest SEZ in China. The purpose behind the construction of these SEZs was to attract foreign investment, upgrade technology, and foster business cooperation with the international business community. In order to achieve this goal, the central government granted more institutional and policy autonomy to the SEZs, enabling foreign and private companies in the SEZs to enjoy such favorable schemes as tax reduction and free use of land. Within a few years, these SEZs achieved great success. Shenzhen, for example, as one of the first four SEZs, quickly transformed from a small village into a modern city and is known in China today as the second Hong Kong.

A billboard of Deng Xiaoping in Shenzhen
(Photo courtesy of Steven Mon)

Two More Economic Hubs: Yangtze River Delta and Bohai Bay Rim

Reforms in other areas also began, although at varying pace of develop-ment. In 1992, Deng Xiaoping visited southern China, including the SEZs in Shenzhen and Zhuhai, and made speeches along the way to reassert his economic reform policy. Later in the year, Deng's economic agenda was legalized within the Communist Party and China took new strides in its overall economic development. In the late 1990s, the government started to develop Shanghai Pudong Economic Development Area (SPEDA) in the Yangtze River Delta, quickly turning this area into the most developed region in the country. With this success, the government then decided to develop the Tianjin Binhai New Area (TBNA) close to Beijing in the Bohai Bay Rim with the hope of developing this area into another economic hub as important as the Pearl River Delta and Yangtze River Delta regions. These three coastal regions connect and function together as the country's economic hubs.

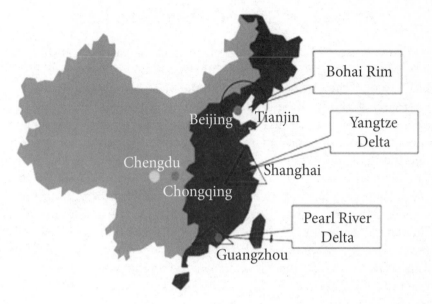

China's three coastal economic hubs

New Strategic Focus: Revitalizing the Northeast and Developing Inland West

Following this regional development model, the Chinese government recently announced a new plan to revitalize and transform the Northeast Region into China's fourth economic powerhouse, after the above three economic hubs. Traditionally, Northeast China was a heavy-industrial base established during the Mao era. A large number of state-owned enterprises are situated here, including steel plants, ore mines, oil refineries, and shipyards. During the decades of economic reforms, the region fell behind other regions due to the inherent low efficiency of state-owned companies and ill-defined product structure. Now the central government is determined to change the situation by transforming the region into another vital industry base during the 11th Five-Year Period (2006–2010).

In addition, the central government is beginning to focus on the inland region of Western China, historically a poor and neglected region inhabited by many minority groups. With the blueprint to establish a "new western China" by the middle of the 21st century, the state has rolled out extensive infrastructure projects and come up with favorable investment measures to attract foreign and domestic investors.

REFORM OF STATE-OWNED ENTERPRISES

In a broad sense, China's economic reform over the past 30 years has been a process of privatizing and reforming the State-Owned Enterprises (SOE), the product of the planned economy in the Mao era.

Strictly speaking, the pre-reform SOEs were not real enterprises but production units under the control of the government. They had no autonomy to decide what and how to produce, acting only as policy executors. They had no worries about going bankrupt and hence no incentive to expand. In addition, they provided their employees with lifetime job guarantees (the so-called iron rice bowl system) and "from-cradle-to-grave" benefits, including housing, healthcare, childcare, education, retirement, and funeral expenses. Understandably, employees had no incentive to work hard. As a result of all these factors, the efficiency and productivity of the SOEs were extremely low, many surviving on government protection and subsidies, like cheap raw materials and low interest loans from state banks.

In the early 1980s, a step-by-step approach to reform the SOEs started. To begin with, SOEs were granted greater autonomy to decide their own production plans based on market needs. Once they had fulfilled the state production quotas, they were able to keep part of the profits in order to expand production. Staring in the mid 1980s, the government began to differentiate the roles of government and enterprises in an effort to separate the right to own and the right to operate. Some poorly operated SOEs were allowed to declare bankruptcy. In 1992, SOEs were given more self-control, including setting prices for their own products and having the right to hire and fire workers. By the end of 1998, thanks to these measures, almost 80% of all SOEs had gone through total or partial privatization.

In 2002, the government made another substantial shift in SOE reform. With the exception of a small number of "lifeline" SOEs that must be wholly state owned, all SOEs had to introduce a joint-stock system, establish effective corporate governance, and operate independently of government control. As a result, those SOEs that consistently ran at a loss were forced to exit the state-owned sector by means of bankruptcy or an infusion of private and foreign capital. They became non-state-owned enterprises or enterprises in which the state was an ordinary shareholder. Some large SOEs formed group companies through mergers and acquisitions, several becoming public companies. This latest step in SOE reform is still underway.

CASE STUDY

How ownership restructuring took place within China's SOEs.

Case 1:

Hainan Airlines is a large SOE. The government approved the sale of a 25% stake to American Aviation Investment with the provision that it would help the airline "study" foreign management and technology. The rest of the shareholders are state institutions (56%), the government (4%), and other individuals (15%).
(*Source:* www.worldbank.org, 2001)

Case 2:

The Changchun-based First Automotive Works Group (FAW) was a heavy burden on the government with staff redundancies reaching 100,000 in 1998. It entered a joint-venture merger with Toyota and re-established itself as a giant Chinese corporation. The merger was the biggest in the history of China's automobile history. Employee numbers were cut by 80%. Its profits increased sixfold by 2001.
(*Source:* http://english.hanban.edu.cn/english/2002/Sep/42820.htm)

THE OPEN-DOOR POLICY

China has been implementing an open-door policy to the outside world, in parallel with the internal state-owned enterprise reform and nationwide privatization process. The adoption of this policy was also a gradual process, facilitated by China's entry into the World Trade Organization (WTO) in 2001. The process includes allowing domestic companies to participate in foreign trade, lifting the trade quota, gradually reducing trade barriers, and increasingly relying on market mechanisms for regulating trade processes. China has benefited significantly as an international trade partner, as can evidently be seen in its increased exports and the ubiquity of made-in-China commodities all over the world.

As early as the 1980s, China began to attract foreign direct investment (FDI) with foreign businesses investing and operating in the newly established Special Economic Zones. Since then, China has seen a rapid increase of inward FDI (see Table 2.2) thanks to the gradual expansion of FDI-oriented open policies beyond the first four SEZs to the whole country. The policies range from approving joint ventures to allowing wholly foreign-owned enterprises, from tightening control of foreign exchange to making RMB convertible on current account, and from offering tax incentives to granting national treatment. Today, FDI plays an important role in China's economy, accounting for 27% of value-added production, 4.1% of national tax revenue, and more than 58% of foreign trade. Companies from 190 countries and regions have invested in China, including 450 of the world's Fortune 500 companies. In 2001, the government began to encourage Chinese companies to invest overseas by means of mergers and acquisitions with foreign companies (for example, Lenovo acquiring IBM's PC business in 2004) and directly operating abroad (for example, Haier set up a factory in the USA). In 2006, China's overall inward FDI totaled $69.5 billion, and the outward flow grew by 32% to $16.1 billion.

CRITICAL ISSUES THAT NEED TO BE ADDRESSED

China has made remarkable achievements over the past 30 years, however, problems have also surfaced as by-products of reform, some serious enough to threaten the sustainability of China's economic development and its social and political stability. The following is a brief summary of these problems, the measures the government has taken, and our suggestions for foreign investors.

Regional Disparity

China's coastal provinces have developed much faster than interior areas, creating great disparities in terms of per capita income between regions. For example, Guangzhou's 2006 GDP per capita was $11,000 whereas the national average was only about $2,000. The government has taken measures to address regional gaps by initiating grand programs to revitalize the Northwest and develop the West. This may represent a good opportunity for foreign businesses since the market in coastal regions is now saturated and extremely competitive. Investing in less developed areas may entail more favorable conditions in terms of tax and land use and win more government support.

Layoffs in State-Owned Enterprises

From the case-study example of the Changchun-based First Automotive Works Group you can see that about 80% of its original employees lost their jobs because of the SOE reform. SOE layoffs have become

Table 2.2 Foreign direct investment in China (total and US): 1998–2007

Total Foreign Direct Investment (FDI)

	1998	1999	2000	2001	2002	2003	2004	2005	2006	2007
No. of Contracts*	19,799	16,918	22,347	26,139	34,171	41,081	43,664	44,019	41,485	37,888
Amount Contracted (US$ billion)	52.10	41.22	62.38	69.20	82.77	115.07	153.48	189.07	200.17	...
Amount Utilized (US$ billion)	45.46	40.32	40.72	46.88	52.74	53.51	60.63	60.33	69.47**	82.66**
US Direct Investment										
No. of Contracts	2,238	2,028	2,609	2,594	3,363	4,060	3,925	3,741	3,205	2,627
Amount Contracted (US$ billion)	6.48	6.02	8.00	7.51	8.20	10.16	12.17	...*	...*	...*
Amount Utilized (US$ billion)	3.90	4.22	4.38	4.86	5.40	4.20	3.94	3.06	3.00	2.62
US Share of Utilized Investment	8.50%	10.47%	10.76%	10.37%	10.24%	7.85%	6.50%	5.07%	4.12%	3.50%

Source: Ministry of Commerce (MOFCOM) and US-China Business Council, http://www.uschina.org/statistics/fdi_cumulative.html.
Notes: * MOFCOM stopped reporting contracted foreign investment figures by country in December 2005. Beginning in 2005, the number of contracts refers to the number of projects and the contracted value refers to actual investment levels.
** Beginning in 2006, FDI statistics explicitly include financial and non-financial FDI; the figure cited incorporates both categories.

a nationwide concern, especially in areas with a large number of state-owned enterprises, such as Northeastern China. Over the past decade or so, the government has struggled to sustain adequate job creation for retrenched workers, migrant labor from rural areas, and fresh college graduates. Government measures include increasing the pace of economic development in less developed areas, improving the social security system, implementing an early retirement plan (age 50 for women and 55 for men in most sectors), and calling for the building of a harmonious society. All levels of government encourage foreign and private companies to create more job opportunities. You can take this factor into consideration when drafting a business plan for your China endeavor.

Income Gap

The issue of income gap is related to retrenchments and the need for adequate jobs. One of the results of rapid economic development is the creation of a group of wealthy people and a small middle-class population in urban areas. China is therefore witnessing a large disparity in terms of people's income. For example, the 2006 average income in Beijing was RMB 17,653, while in the poorer Qinghai Province it was only RMB 8,057. Rural residents earn only 25% of the average urban resident's income. The richest 10% of Chinese families own 40% of all private assets. The top 20% account for 50% of total income or spending, while the poorest 20% take home only 4.7%.

Corruption

Corrupt practices are another serious social problem with a number of high-ranking officials involved. This is closely related to bribery, gray income, inequality, abuse of power, and economic crimes. To cope with the problem, the government has taken a series of legislative measures, however their effectiveness is questionable. The central government has also called for high-ranking officials to cultivate higher moral standards by following a Confucian code of conduct. (We will come back to this topic in the next chapter.)

Environment

Deterioration in the environment has become a long-term threat to China's growth and sustainability due to over-rapid economic development and accelerated urbanization. The government has taken legislative measures but with seemingly little effect. This is a concern you should keep in mind when deciding in which sector or area to invest in China. Foreign companies whose production processes harm the environment will not obtain start-up approval in China.

DOING BUSINESS IN CHINA: CHALLENGES AND OPPORTUNITIES

Over the past three decades, large numbers of foreign companies have jumped on the bandwagon by investing and operating in China, many achieving great success. These companies have taken advantage of China's low-cost labor, favorable tax and land use policies, huge market, and social stability, together with their own comparative advantages in terms of capital, technology, brand names, and international experience.

Even so, these foreign companies have experienced and will continue to experience many challenges in China, including administrative interference, operational restraints, lack of a complete legal system, intense local competition, cultural differences, to name a few. However, opportunities often go hand-in-hand with challenges. The issue is how to bypass and/or cope with challenges while maximizing opportunities. You will need to consider the pros and cons of doing business in China, taking into account the challenges listed below and working toward a viable balance.

Business Sector

First of all, you should know that foreign companies are not permitted to directly operate a business in China. Governmental approval is required for establishing a firm with an element of foreign investment, whether wholly owned or partnered. The possibility of gaining approval and the percentage of foreign equity holding allowed depend on the industry sector involved. Business sectors are classified as: encouraged, permitted, restricted, and prohibited, though there is no clear boundary between these categories. Therefore, the business sector you choose will directly affect the outcome of government review as to your investment plan and the allowed percentage of your equity holding. Generally speaking, businesses that are more welcome include those adopting new technologies, meeting market needs, and saving energy and raw materials. Restricted businesses include those applying technology that is slow to develop, resource-intensive, and harmful to the environment. You therefore need to plan carefully in order to get approval and win more government support.

Forms of Investment

There are different forms of FDI in China, each subject to different regulations formulated by the government (see Appendix C for details). One important decision you need to make when entering the Chinese market is whether you need a local partner. There are pros and cons for either decision. For now we will use the joint-venture option as an illustration.

If you choose to set up a joint venture with a Chinese company, it may be easier to bypass governmental restrictions since your partner can help secure licenses and approvals. This is vital since China today still lacks a transparent administrative process and a fully functioning legal system. Other advantages include convenience in obtaining a local market share, a distribution network, and local resources, such as land, raw materials, energy, utilities, and transportation. This option is especially advantageous for small and medium companies that don't have enough resources and business experience in China. In addition, joint-venture is often preferred by the Chinese government since it can help save local SOEs from bankruptcy, create more employment opportunities, and reduce competition with local companies.

On the down side, joint-ventures may make it difficult to control the business and cause possible management disputes with local partners due to differences in corporate culture, divergent business experiences, disagreement in technology transfer, violations of intellectual property rights, and so on.

Investment Location

Another concurrent decision you need to make is where you should invest in the vast land of China. You can choose to go to the developed areas along the coast in the three economic hubs or their surrounding areas. Or you can choose to go to less developed areas, such as the inland western and northwestern regions. You need to balance the pros and cons.

If you choose to go to the coastal areas you will enjoy better infrastructure and human capital, higher government efficiency, and a relatively transparent market. Simply put, you will experience fewer risks. But fewer risks also mean fewer opportunities since the markets in these areas tend to be saturated and highly competitive.

If you choose to invest in less developed areas, the government will be very pleased and give you more support and expediency. You will enjoy more favorable conditions, such as tax reduction and cheaper land use, and encounter less intense market competition. But the pros you may enjoy if choosing the well-developed areas will turn to cons here, for example, inconvenient transportation and incompetent local government.

Other Areas that May Boost Your Success

You have probably realized by now that in China the government plays an important role in the success of a foreign business. So a solid relationship is a must: this is known as *guanxi*. However, as we will emphasize again and again in the rest of the book, *guanxi* does not simply mean bribing government officials. You can use other means to establish and maintain a quality *guanxi* as a way to win government support. First of all, you can do some research on possible problems the local government needs to address. Then you can see if you will be able to help solve the problems through establishing and developing your business in the area. If it is a possibility, let the government know what you can do, how you can do it, and what you can achieve in both the short term and the long term. For example, you can agree to hire more local workers to help relieve the unemployment burden of the local government. You can state in the investment plan how you can promote or at least not damage the environment. You can also help stimulate the local economy by using local suppliers and distributors and increasing exports in the near future. Remember, a win-win situation is what you should convey to the government and what you should target.

SUMMARY

While the Japanese and American economies are struggling in the doldrums, the Chinese economy remains buoyant and less reliant on exports. At the First Session of the 11th National People's Congress (NPC) held from March 5–18, 2008, the Chinese government predicted more healthy growth figures (see Table 2.1). The figures are based on responses of executives from the world's top 1,000 companies to a survey which asked about future direct investments. According to the World Bank, by 2020 China's share of world trade will have more than tripled to 10%. Using the purchasing power parity method of calculating global output, China will be the second largest economy in the world with 8% of the world's total, second only to the USA (Chan 2003, 267–268). In the decade to come, China's economy may act as a spark to keep the global economic engine moving and buttress the slowdown in other markets, such as Japan and the USA. Therefore, Chinese economic development will not only benefit China but the whole world. You and your company should be part of it.

Part Two

Why the Chinese are Chinese

3 Understanding Chinese Mentality (I)

From the first two chapters you have gained some background knowledge on China. In this chapter we focus more on the people you will work with. You may already have learned that the Chinese are a polite and hospitable people, perhaps from movies, novels, or the experience of others. But sometimes the Chinese can appear unfathomable. In the same vein, your Chinese partner may also find you difficult to fathom from time to time. To help you understand the reasons behind these cultural differences, this chapter introduces to you Confucius, the most important figure in Chinese history, and Confucianism, the philosophy that has shaped almost all aspects of Chinese culture. Case studies, observations, and suggestions will help you be more aware of the attitudes you come across in China today.

CONFUCIUS AND CONFUCIANISM

Confucius (551 BC–479 BC) is the Latinized form of Kong Fuzi, literally meaning "Kong the Master" in Chinese. Confucius is regarded as the most influential educator, thinker, and philosopher in Chinese history.

Confucius lived in the Spring and Autumn Period (722 BC–481 BC) when China experienced the transition from a slave society to a feudalistic society. The country began to grow so big that the king could not centrally control all his territory and the nation fell apart into several states. Needless to say, it was a period of turbulence, chaos, and endless wars. Intellectuals of the time were concerned about the future mode of society and proposed different political and ideological ideals aimed at ending social upheaval and achieving political unity. Confucius was one such intellectual. He traveled from state to state, advocating his philosophy, although none of the rulers would accept his virtue-based way of ruling a state. He returned home in old age and spent the rest of his life teaching students. His thoughts were later recorded by his followers in *The Analects of Confucius*.

Unlike most Western philosophers, Confucius did not rely on deductive reasoning but used analogy and aphorisms to explain his ideas. Mencius (372 BC–289 BC) and a few others further developed his philosophy largely through argumentation and reasoning. Thus Confucianism is also called *Kong-Meng Zhi Dao* ("The Way of Confucius and Mencius") in Chinese.

During the Qin Dynasty (221 BC–206 BC), the first unified empire in Chinese history, Emperor Qin Shihuang adopted a legalist form of government and outlawed Confucianism along with other schools of thought. He ordered about 400 Confucian scholars buried alive lest they subvert his legalism-based rule. It was not until the reign of Emperor Wu (156 BC–87 BC), during the Han Dynasty (206 BC–AD 9), that Confucianism was first established as the state ideology. The emperor believed that only strict followers of the Confucian code could become moral and honest officials and help him run the country. From then on, Confucianism became the core of the civil service examinations through which government officials were selected.

In the dynasties following the Han period, Confucianism remained part of the mainstream Chinese orthodoxy, despite its loss of dominance during the Tang Dynasty (618–907) when Daoism had a greater influence. During the Song Dynasty (960–1279), however, a school of Neo-Confucianism represented by Zhu Xi (1130–1200) helped restore the dominant role of Confucianism by integrating some Daoist and Buddhist ideas. Confucianism maintained its dominant position for the next 700 years until the early 20th century. Confucianism also became the state philosophy in Korea, Vietnam, and Japan.

During his lifetime, Confucius tried to bring social and civil order in the midst of social upheaval. Basically, his thoughts discourage social change or revolution. For this reason, Confucianism was attacked as being at the core of the old political and cultural system during the May Fourth

Movement (1919). For the same reason, it was banned by the Chinese government for many years after the founding of the People's Republic of China, especially during the Cultural Revolution (1966–1976).

In China today, despite the fact that Communism has been held as the belief system for nearly 60 years, Confucianism remains deeply rooted in people's lives, influencing the way in which the Chinese view the world and guide their attitudes towards family, authority, and interpersonal relationships. In the same vein, people in business environments are unconsciously functioning in a Confucian manner and following the Confucian code of conduct in their dealings with business partners and competitors. Therefore, if you want to have smooth business transactions and work comfortably with your Chinese counterpart, you should understand Confucian fundamentals in order to figure out why the Chinese conduct their day-to-day business in certain ways.

PRINCIPLES OF CONFUCIANISM

The tenets of Confucianism are *Ren* and *Li*. The Chinese character for *Ren* (仁) is composed of two parts: "human being" and "two," which implies the importance of relationships in people's lives. There are five pairs of relationships that determine people's position with each other: ruler and subject; father and son; elder brother and younger brother; husband and wife; and friend and friend according to age. *Li* refers to the morality, etiquette, customs, and rituals that people, including rulers, should uphold in order to function well in society. Simply put, *Ren* emphasizes social relationships and *Li* focuses on the individual's moral conduct and restraint. Below, we elaborate on how *Ren* and *Li* may be achieved and function in the life of the Chinese.

Family–A Basic Social Unit

Confucianism places great value on family, the pre-eminent unit in one's life. Family is a mini-kingdom where the parents rule, set an example for their children on how to function as members, and educate their children to become moral and respectful people. Children in turn learn to behave according to their role in the family so that they can act accordingly in society, the extended form of the family. For example, the young should respect the elder, and women should obey men. To distinguish positions in this kinship web, special terms have been invented in the Chinese language to refer to different family members: elder brother, younger brother, older sister, and younger sister. There are specific titles for different kinds of

Four generations in an extended family

uncle: older paternal uncle, younger maternal uncle, or paternal younger uncle who is the cousin of the father, and so on.

In a traditional family, the basic rule was filial piety (*xiào*), which is the household equivalent of having to respect those who are superior in society. In general terms, filial piety means respecting one's parents, taking care of them when they are old, making sure that male heirs carry on the family name (no longer true under the one-child policy), bringing honor to the family by achieving social status, displaying sorrow for parents' sickness and death, and carrying out sacrifices after their death. Filial piety is considered the first virtue in Chinese culture. There are many historical instances of how people upheld filial piety in extreme circumstances.

FYI

In China today, many Chinese still believe that a person cannot be a loyal friend as well as an excellent employee unless he or she is a dutiful son or daughter. Filial piety is therefore sometimes used as a criterion to judge a person. It is said that some Chinese companies hire employees based on this standard in addition to other criteria. With this aspect of Chinese culture in mind, you should be careful when talking about your relationship with your parents. It is one of the ways to judge if you are a responsible and reliable business partner.

In many ways the Chinese view themselves more as part of a family rather than an independent individual. This can be mirrored in the order of a Chinese name: the family name comes before the given name. The wellbeing of each individual member is closely related to the family as a whole. For example, if one succeeds outside, that person will bring honor or "face" to the whole family. Thus, Chinese parents attach great importance to their children's education since the success of their children bears directly on their own honor. Everyone should have a family in the eyes of most Chinese people. If somebody reaches a certain age and still remains single, people may consider him or her strange and the parents will push him or her to get married as soon as possible.

FYI

Family is often a topic of daily conversation and small talk before serious business negotiations. By doing this, people get to know each other better and ease the relationship. Even though this may conflict with your notion of respecting the privacy of others, it is necessary that you show an interest in the family of your Chinese partners. You can ask after his or her parents and where his or her children go to school. If you have a chance to meet with his family, don't forget to compliment them on their excellent achievement. By doing so, you can substantially narrow the gap between you and the Chinese side and pave the way for upcoming business deals. In return, you should expect to be asked about your family: if you are married, how many children you have, who takes care of your aging parents, and so on. Please bear in mind that it is a token of goodwill from your Chinese friends rather than an intrusion into your private life.

Collectivism vs. Individualism

Today, as in earlier, traditional China, social groups can be regarded as an extension of the Confucian notion of family. Social groups include the workplace and the country, the largest group of all. In Chinese the unit word used for a company, school, and department store is *jia* (family). The formal word for "country" is a combination of the characters "country" and "family" (*guojia*). "Big family" (*dajia*) refers to everybody present. Familial forms of address, such as uncle, elder sister, or brother, are often used to address co-workers according to age, if they have no official or professional titles. Traditionally, the person who ruled a local area was referred to as the "parental official" (*fu mu guan*). The plural form of "we" and "us" is often used to refer to oneself instead of "I" and "me." In other words, Chinese culture is based on the concept of collectivism.

The corollary to this is that collectivist social groups should provide support to their members when necessary. For example, the workplace, as a second home, should take care of its members financially and psychologically. This was particularly true from the founding of the PRC till the economic reforms in 1978. The work unit guaranteed its employees job security (the iron rice bowl system mentioned in Chapter 2) and provided almost free housing and medical care. The company would even be responsible for looking for a spouse for its employees if somebody was still single beyond a certain age. In return, an individual would place the interests of the social group above his or her own needs.

Before the economic reforms got underway, people were simply told which college they would go to, what job they would be assigned to, and what kind of apartment they would live in. Individualism was connected with selfishness and was open to criticism. Simply put, at that time people were educated to be loyal to the country and the Communist Party.

Today, however, things have changed. People have a lot more freedom to choose their own careers and follow their preferred lifestyle, especially well-educated young people in large cities. But among older people and people in power, family values and altruism still remain an acclaimed virtue by which promotion decisions are usually made in government agencies and state-owned enterprises.

Behave Accordingly

Confucius believed that a society will be blessed with peace and prosperity when everyone knows his or her place, understands his or her obligations to others in the hierarchy, and seeks to perfect his or her role. This "everyone" includes both the ruler and the ruled, as aptly summarized in one of his well-known quotations, "Let the ruler be a ruler, the subject be a subject, the father be a father, and the son be a son."

Within a social organization, the person who rules usually acts more like a father figure. He should manage his subordinates with compassion and love rather than merely by rules and regulations. He should set an example for the people under him and behave with the highest moral integrity. He should care for the private wellbeing of his subordinates, including even their marriage problems. In return, his people should serve him with respect and loyalty. In this way, stability and harmony can be maintained and the organization can function better.

If you are going to work in China as a manager and lead a group of Chinese employees, you should express your care and concern for your subordinates. Your mindfulness will be rewarded with their respect and loyalty, contributing to internal harmony and the success of the business.

Bow to Rank, Title, and Experience

China is still a hierarchical society. One's age, title, and rank announce where a person stands in relation to others in society. Thus "naming" or giving people the right title is important in Confucian ideology. You may find that many Chinese address others and like to be addressed by their official and professional titles, even among neighbors or close friends. Those who don't use the correct form of address are considered impolite and disrespectful. As a foreigner, you may be excused for not following the code, but if you do, you will gain yourself a lot of credits. However, if you address someone by the wrong title, especially a lower title, the person will feel offended. Try your best to learn who is who.

Because of the structural hierarchy, you may find that it takes longer to make a decision in China than you are used to, especially in state-owned enterprises and government agencies. What may seem like an easy decision to you may in China be made by a group of people after an extended discussion. If you find that your business counterpart sounds vague or hesitant toward a simple matter, it is often because he or she does not have the power to decide or doesn't want to take the responsibility for the decision without consulting with a superior. The following example will help explain.

CASE STUDY

Why did Mr. Li seek Mr. Wu's nod?

An American—let's call him Mr. Jones—was interested in importing porcelain coffee mugs and noodle bowls from Guangxi. He went to the factory to make the deal, negotiating very hard with Mr. Li, the deputy manager in charge of imports and exports. Just as Mr. Li nodded agreement to the price terms and quantity, Mr. Wu, a senior deputy manager, walked into the room. Mr. Li then respectfully consulted Mr. Wu on every detail of what had already been agreed upon with Mr. Jones. Mr. Li told Mr. Jones that the agreement they had just reached was not final, at which point Mr. Jones thought the deal might go sour. The next morning, Mr. Li called Mr. Jones, saying that the agreement was still valid. Mr. Li explained that, even though he had the same authority in making decisions as Mr. Wu, it was the custom that he should give face to Mr. Wu because he was Mr. Li's senior in terms of age. If Mr. Li had made a unilateral decision he would have offended Mr. Wu.

In China, age is related to experience and wisdom, so an older age is accorded respect. An elder man is addressed as *Lao* (old) preceded by his last name, such as Li Lao and Chen Lao, to show respect. At banquets, elders sit at the best place and are the first to be served. When passing through a door, one should let the elder person go first. Sometimes one even makes a show of it by saying, "You're older; you should go first" or "You're the manager; you go first." So older people in China don't have any need to hide their age and sometimes just tell you their age without being asked.

China is undergoing dramatic social transformations. Some traditional values only hold true for some occasions. For example, Confucianism holds that an older person is more experienced, wiser, and thus superior to younger people. Hence, the Chinese expect to do business with someone older in age and higher in title. Older people receive respect and are taken care of by the family. On the other hand, age discrimination is seen everywhere in the country. Woman in their early 40s are forced to retire from some state-owned enterprises and age requirements are clearly stated in job advertisements. If you happen to work with a high-tech company or private company, you may find the people with whom you work are very young.

FYI

The Chinese tend to apply the same approach to foreigners in terms of age, title, and rank. They are very particular about the rank, title, age, and the decision-making power of the person doing business with them. We are told that a cooperative business program was dropped by a Chinese company simply because the person sent by the foreign side was too young to be trusted. As the saying goes, "Like meets like," the higher your status, the higher-ranking officials you can meet. Therefore, it is important to send someone with the highest credentials possible, especially in your company's first attempt to do business in China. You can gain entry much easier, meet more important people, and come back home with more important decisions. This also applies to the standing of the company in national and international markets. The Chinese want to work with the best. If your firm does not have the status, you will have to double your effort and make more concessions to win the deal.

Virtuous Humility and Modesty

Many Westerners find that when they give a sincere compliment to a Chinese, more often than not they will hear denial in return, with a typical reply like "*Bu hao, bu hao!*" (Not good, not good!) or "*Nali, nali!*" (Far from being that good!). When you are invited to a magnificent banquet, you may often hear the Chinese host comment with an apologetic tone that they have not prepared enough food, when the table is actually overflowing with eight, ten, and even more beautifully presented, mouth-watering dishes. To most Westerners, such responses may sound dishonest, ungrateful, or impolite. But to the Chinese, responding to a compliment with thanks or other acknowledgments of its validity goes against the value of humility, one of the most prized virtues among the Chinese.

As professors teaching at American universities, we are often asked by our fellow faculty members to explain why students from China are reluctant to raise their hands in class and participate in class discussions. These students have been taught not to call attention to one's self or family, but to seek anonymity in the masses. Chinese rarely talk about their achievements or show self-satisfaction, even though their accomplishments are visible. They may be excessively self-deprecating, to a degree that makes you question their sincerity and honesty. By doing this the Chinese make themselves more invisible in the group and minimize the damage to the original balance in the relationship with other people because of his or her achievement or promotion in title and rank.

In this way, the Chinese tend to play themselves down while Americans tend to play themselves up. If you want to get a job in the United States, you should tell people at the job interview how capable you are. Sometimes you even have to boast a little in order to get the position. But in China, you should play yourself down and need to say something like: "I have some knowledge or experience in the field, but it is very limited. All of you can be my teachers. I will work hard and learn from you." The approach is different, but the desired result is the same. You want people to act in your favor.

Today China's younger generation may go against the above tradition. They are more individualistic, self-centered, articulate, and less modest. Nevertheless, they tend to act in a more traditional way if attending interviews and seeking promotion, especially in government organizations and state-owned companies.

For you, a non-Chinese, our advice is that when you interact with Chinese people it's best if you can weave a sense of humility, modesty, and

Bow to authority

self-negation into your comments and speech. This, of course, may not be easy for some Westerners who have grown up in a culture that upholds individualism. But what you gain may be worth the effort.

FYI

It is well known that the Chinese are polite, modest, and courteous, but from time to time you may find the opposite, that someone is rude and uncaring by any standard. For example, some people don't queue to get on a bus; no apologies or thanks are given when doing something wrong or receiving a favor; few people hold the door for the people behind. Over population is one reason for such contradictory phenomena. Another explanation is that people can present themselves differently in different settings: being polite and modest within his social groups and rude and uncaring outside. We will discuss this in detail in the chapter on *guanxi*.

Recognize Personal Effort

As seen from the above, the uneven distribution of power in Chinese society places individuals in different positions within the social hierarchy. An individual will have more respect, pride, and dignity if he can successfully move up the social ladder. This is also why Confucius emphasizes education and personal effort. According to Confucianism, access to power should not be determined by birthright or class but through education and personal effort (*you jiao wu lei*). In ancient times the imperial civil service examination was used to select those who made the greatest personal efforts through education to win official positions. Talented young men from both rich and poor families studied Confucian classics, practiced the writing of pre-styled expository articles, and took examinations. If they passed, they would become government officials. As a result, they would be highly respected as exemplary figures for people in the surrounding area and their families would rise in prestige and wealth as well. Thus, the maxim of "Study well and become an official" (*xue er you ze shi*) was the ultimate goal.

Chinese students attending American universities are regarded as the most hard-working and highest-achieving group of students. The significance given to rank and title in Confucian ideology explains their diligence in study and work, since this can be exchanged for respect, prestige, and wealth, which in turn bring glory to the family. In this sense, the Chinese are also a competitive people.

FYI

The Chinese imperial examination system began around the sixth century with the justification that appointees to civil service positions should not be chosen through inherited privilege but through individual abilities. There were three levels of examination: local, provincial, and national. The exams tested the examinees on their knowledge of the Confucian classics, ability to compose articles and poems, calligraphy, and critical thinking about contemporary social and political issues. The examination at the provincial level could last up to 72 hours. Those who passed the local level gained the title *Xiucai*, the provincial level *Juren*, and the national level *Jinshi*. The pass rate was very low, about 2% in the Tang Dynasty. Records show that almost half of the successful candidates were from families with no connections. For many talented young people, passing the exams was the only way to change their lives and bring wealth and prestige to their family. Since the pass rate was so low, many candidates spent almost all their lives preparing for and taking the exams. The examination system was abolished in 1905 shortly before the fall of the Qing Dynasty.

In the work place one's title and rank will change over time. An individual's movement up and down the hierarchy can easily cause resentment and hurt feelings among others. Confucianism therefore recognizes personal efforts to move up the hierarchy and also the need to instruct people to follow the necessary rules of conduct in order to accord respect to different positions within the hierarchy. In this way, relationships can be balanced and rebalanced and social harmony achieved. This is why self-cultivation and self-discipline are essential components of human behavior, without which harmony cannot prevail. With this in mind, people should avoid confrontation, maintain their temper, not raise their voice, and smile rather than appear angry.

Fighting their way up the social ladder

CONFUCIANISM IN CHINA TODAY

As mentioned at the beginning of the chapter, Confucianism was practically banned during the time between the founding of the PRC and the economic reforms in 1978. Nevertheless, Confucianism has been invited back in recent years, not as the state ideology but as a means to govern the country. The former Chinese President, Jiang Zemin, while in office stated that China should be both regulated by Confucian moral values and ruled by laws and regulations. The central government has called on high-ranking officials to study the thoughts of Confucius in order to discipline their behavior. China's only national TV station, CCTV, produces a program in which famous scholars use everyday Chinese to illustrate *The Analects of Confucius*. On the international front, Confucius and his thoughts are being employed as an icon of 5,000 years of Chinese culture and so far over 200 Confucius Institutes have been set up worldwide, with the support of the Chinese government.

There are reasons behind this. According to He Qinglian (He 1998), the market-oriented economy has replaced the socialist planned economy in China and as a result the old Communist or socialist ideology that calls for people to sacrifice individual interests for the collectivist goal is no longer convincing to the people. Without a replacement ideology and moral code to function in the new market-oriented economy, many people are at a loss as to what is moral and what is immoral. As a consequence, corruption and economic crimes are reported everywhere and people just want to get rich by whatever means possible. A set of moral code to regulate people's behavior is highly necessary, especially in the gray areas between the legal and illegal. Confucian thoughts can be borrowed for this purpose.

On the other hand, with the rapid economic growth over the past 30 years, the egalitarian society established by Mao Zedong between 1949 and 1976 has been replaced by a widening gap between the rich and poor. While the wealthy plan their summer trips to northern Europe, the poor are worried about how to survive in a competitive society. Dissatisfaction, complaints, and criticism can always be heard. To sustain the development that has been achieved over the past few decades, the central government has made calls to build a stable and peaceful society. So harmony, the core principle in Confucianism, is one of the most frequently used words in government speeches and the slogan "To build a harmonious society" can be found and heard everywhere. To achieve this, Chinese President Hu Jintao has stipulated the concept of "Eight Honors and Eight Disgraces" as the new moral yardstick to measure the work and conduct of government officials and ordinary people. Here is its English translation:

Love the country; do it no harm.
Serve the people; never betray them.
Follow science; discard superstition.
Be diligent; not indolent.
Be united, help each other; make no gains at others' expense.
Be honest and trustworthy; do not squander ethics for profit.
Be disciplined and law-abiding; not chaotic and lawless.
Live plainly, work hard; do not wallow in luxuries and pleasure.

Chapter

4 Understanding Chinese Mentality (II)

I n this chapter we continue our discussion on why the Chinese are Chinese by introducing two more iconic figures in Chinese history and their doctrines: Lao Zi and Daoism, and Sun Zi and *The Art of War*. Both were contemporaries of Confucius and lived in a period of political upheaval. Each developed a school of thought that has deeply influenced the mentality of the Chinese in general and the way business is conducted in particular.

LAO ZI AND DAOISM

Lao Zi, meaning Old Master, was reportedly older than Confucius. Like Confucius, Lao Zi was a great philosopher who founded Daoism (Taoism), one of the two great philosophical traditions along with Confucianism. Lao Zi's philosophy was summed up in *Dao De Jing* (*Classic of the Way and Virtue*), the first philosophical work in Chinese history. In this little book of about 5,000 characters, Lao Zi presented his philosophical thoughts in a concise, comprehensive, and profound manner. However, historians are divided over whether Lao Zi was a real person or just a legendary figure and whether *Dao De Jing* was written by himself or a group of people.

FYI

Daoism as an English term corresponds to both *Daojia* as a school of philosophical thought expounded by Lao Zi and Zhuang Zi, another influential Chinese Daoist, and *Daojiao* "teaching of the *Dao*" as a religion. Thus, "Daoism" in English encompasses thought and practice; it sometimes is viewed as "philosophical," sometimes as "religious," and at other times as a combination of both. According to historical sources, about 700 years after Lao Zi's death, a group of people developed a religion called Daoism around Lao Zi's ideas in order to meet the need of ordinary people for a god to worship in their life. Religious Daoists worshiped gods of the earth and heaven, ancestors and dragons, gods of seasons, and god of the kitchen. Some Daoist followers made pills to help live a longer life while others became hermits living close to nature.

Arguably, Lao Zi shared some views with Confucius, such as self-cultivation and worldly concerns. Compared to Confucius, however, Lao Zi developed a more spiritual explanation for the nature of the universe. While Confucius wanted to educate people, name things to distinguish people, and offer solutions to world problems, Lao Zi believed such endeavors were sources of frustration and fragmentation. Instead, people should be *wu wei* or "take no-action," follow *Dao* ("The Way"), and act naturally rather than willfully oppose or tamper with how reality is moving.

Dao—The Way

The central tenet of Lao Zi's philosophy is *Dao*, literally translated as The Way or The Path. *Dao* is a difficult concept. Confucius said, "If I could discover *Dao* in the morning, I would not regret dying in the evening." According to Lao Zi, the underlying order of the world was a mysterious but utterly reliable force or *Dao*. This *Dao* is a universal energetic intelligence that informs and directs all life. *Dao* is unnamed and unknowable yet it is the essential unifying element of all. In other words, everything is basically one thing despite the differences in appearance. Because all is one, matters of good or evil, true or false, as well as differing opinions, can only arise when people lose sight of the oneness as the true nature.

Yin and *Yang*

The collision and collusion between *yin* and *yang* is a good example for illustrating Lao Zi's thought that one is all and all is one. The notion of *yin* refers to the feminine, dark, cold, and passive while *yang* refers to the masculine, light, hot, and active. The combination of one *yin* and one *yang* is the way of nature and the seed of change. *Yin* and *yang* are two forces that are simultaneously opposing and complementing each other. They cannot be separated and should be considered as a whole. In other words, the extreme of *yin* is *yang* and the extreme of *yang* is *yin*. Nowadays, everyone who knows something about Chinese culture is familiar with the image of *yin* and *yang*. It has become a representation of the Chinese view about the world.

FYI

Fengshui, a popular Chinese term in English, is a derivative notion from the Daoist *yin-yang* principle. Fengshui is literally translated as "wind-water," a practice of placement and arrangement of space to achieve harmony with nature. Fengshui practitioners believe that everything contains *qi*, the energy or life force. This *qi* possesses two properties, *yin* (receptive) and *yang* (active)—they are opposites but cannot exist without the other. Within the *qi*, eight constituents compose the universe: the Lake, the Mountain, Fire, Water, Heaven, Thunder, Wind, and Earth. The proper arrangement of these energy qualities will promote both the *qi* of the environment and the *qi* of the individual within the environment, fostering prosperity, health, and wellbeing. Fengshui is very popular in Hong Kong and Macao among businesses and more recently in China. When building an office, for example, the company may hire a fengshui practitioner to determine if the office is in harmony with the universe according to the function of the room and the person who will use the room.

The Middle Way

According to Lao Zi, the key to life is not synthesizing the two forces of *yin* and *yang*; rather it is to find the Way between them, the middle ground, or a compromise. Daoists believe that everything in the universe, including self, family, and business, contain competing tendencies. Avoiding extremes, maintaining a middle path, taking no actions (*wu wei*), and yielding to the natural flow of events can help people survive in an adverse environment and achieve harmony with other people and with nature. Most philosophers believe that *Zhong,* or the "middle way," is the essence of the Chinese view of the world centered on the notion of universal unity. Following this line, some people interpreted the literal meaning of the word China—the Middle Kingdom—as staying in the middle to maintain a balance between divergent forces.

DAOISM, EVERYDAY LIFE, AND BUSINESS PRACTICE

Daoism has a profound impact on the way the Chinese view the world. A lot of people believe that the Chinese in general terms are *"wai ru nei dao,"* meaning that the Chinese follow the Confucian way when interacting with others but turn to the Daoist beliefs for personal aspirations. In other words, from the Confucian doctrines, people learn to behave according to a social role, such as benevolence, courtesy, and respect in order to achieve a harmonious relationship with others. Daoist philosophy, on the other hand, teaches people to maintain an internal balance and follow the natural course especially in times of adversity. Hence, such advice as "Don't take it too seriously" and "Don't be against your fate," can often be heard to comfort others and selves in times of difficulty.

Daoist doctrines exert an important influence on business operations. Zhang Ruimin, CEO of the Haier Group, China's largest and best-known electronics manufacturer, once said in an interview that Confucianism and Daoism have influenced him most, both as a social being and a businessman. According to Wong et al. (1998), for a business operating in the market, *Dao* is actually a "given set of circumstances," "the passive, mystical, intangible, ever-present, ever-changing, totally permeating dynamic." If a business can act in tune with a given situation, it can optimize its performance in the market.

Compared to Western markets, the Chinese market has great potential but is quite different due to its ongoing changes, fledgling legal system, administrative hurdles, and the influence of an old culture. However, if a foreign business is willing to understand China's special characteristics, accept its differences, make efforts to determine its real needs, and show a sincere concern for the interests of the local people, the company should have a promising entry into the market and achieve great success. For example, a foreign company can help the local government solve unemployment problems by creating more job opportunities, boosting export of local products rather than taking away a market share from its Chinese counterparts, and donating money to local schools as a repayment to the local society as a whole.

Some researchers apply Daoist principles in their interpretation of Chinese business negotiation style (Chen 2001). If some foreign businesses complain that it takes too long to negotiate with the Chinese, the explanation would be that the Chinese believe both sides in the negotiation process can be right, even though they disagree with each other. Since the middle way is hard to find, the ritual back-and-forth of haggling is necessary as a means of settling the differences before the best compromise can be found. If successful, a win-win situation is achieved. Based on this explanation, you should know that time and patience are necessary if you want to do business in China.

SUN ZI AND *THE ART OF WAR*

Sun Zi (544 BC–496 BC), Sun the Master, was the author of the earliest and the most revered military treatise in the world, *The Art of War*. Sun Zi, a contemporary of Confucius and Lao Zi, lived about 2,500 years ago in a time of political and military turmoil. Unlike them, he was a military general leading the army to settle disputes and work toward a peaceful society. Based on his rich battlefield experience, Sun Zi wrote *The Art of War*, the most famous book on military strategies and tactics in history.

This book is composed of 13 chapters, each of which is devoted to one aspect of warfare. The influence of Daoism is clear. Its basic principle states: "To win without fighting is best." It is parallel to Lao Zi's *Wu wei* or non-action: use one's wisdom without taking any real action. The *yin-yang* principle also finds its way into Sun Zi's war strategies: if planned and implemented well, *yin* can conquer *yang*, weak can defeat strong, and small can overpower big.

Another fundamental principle in Sun Zi's *The Art of War* is that the general must know everything about the enemy as well as himself, be prepared to both anticipate changing situations and adapt to them whenever they occur. In other words, the general has to have up-to-the-minute intelligence about the opponent and know his own strengths and weaknesses thoroughly. Based on this, he can determine when and how to take advantage of the circumstances to defeat the enemy with as few actions as possible.

Quotations from *The Art of War*

- The best victory is when the opponent surrenders of his own accord before there are any actual hostilities. It is best to win without fighting.

- A military operation involves deception. Even though you are competent, appear to be incompetent. Though effective, appear to be ineffective.

- Rapidity is the essence of war: take advantage of the enemy's unreadiness, make your way by unexpected routes, and attack unguarded positions.

- Move not unless you see an advantage; use not your troops unless there is something to be gained; fight not unless the position is critical.

Reading this far, you may feel confused and puzzled about the contradictory interplay between Confucianism and Sun Zi's battle stratagies in the Chinese mentality since the former values harmonious interpersonal relationships (humanity and virtues) while the latter guides people against others in combat and social interactions (defense and offense). However, some scholars argue that in *The Art of War* Sun Zi assimilated the tenets of Confucianism in a broad sense (Fang 1999). According to Confucianism, if the ruler is not righteous and virtuous, the subjects can revolt and choose a better one. Thus the use of Chinese stratagems against insincere and unrighteous rivals can be morally justified. In terms of face and group interest, a Chinese can defend himself against an opponent's offensive tactics by employing deceptive stratagems if the circumstances require.

Following this line, if two sides do not establish a close *guanxi* at the negotiation table, neither of them has an obligation to be fair but can use strategies and tactics to take advantage of his negotiating counterpart. To build and maintain a *guanxi* network, people can also employ such tactics as interpersonal skills and communication skills. We will elaborate on this point in Chapter 7.

FYI

Chinese history tells a well-known story about a general who confronted his enemies as a Confucian gentleman. Instead of using the best time to attack and defeat his enemy, he waited for them to be fully prepared. His justification was totally Confucian: a gentleman should never attack one who is unprepared and a gentleman should never attack an army which has not yet completed its battle alignment. His troops were defeated as a result and the general himself was seriously wounded.

The Art of War and Doing Business in China

There is a popular Chinese saying in business circles: "To do business is like fighting on the battlefield." Quite a few Chinese business terms are borrowed from military terms, for example, "kill the price," and "march into a market." In *Chinese Business Negotiation Style*, Fang summarizes eight common features between business competition and military battlefields:

1. Both enterprises and armies strive for a favorable position to protect themselves and defeat their opponents.
2. Enterprise competitions and wars are confrontational activities.
3. Both business organizations and military forces must be well organized and managed.
4. Both require strategies and tactics in order to win.
5. The leadership of both an army and an enterprise plays a decisive role in obtaining success.
6. Both rely on high quality and committed people.
7. Both require a supply of resources and logistics.
8. Both attach importance to intelligence gathering and logistics.

(Fang 1999, 77)

Due to these similarities, Sun Zi's stratagems have offered a lot of inspiration and tactics to business operations, including corporate strategy, negotiation tactics, enterprise management, office politics, and more. For example, Sun Zi's *The Art of War* advocates "to win without fighting."

Similarly "the real art of doing business is to succeed without engaging in destructive and cutthroat competition" (Wong et al. 1998). As a foreign business in China, if you want to win the support of the government, try not to compete against your Chinese counterparts, instead engage them in projects which can benefit them as well. Or you can enter sectors that can help China advance in technology and services instead of sectors in which China already has core competence (Wong et al. 1998).

In the business world, the most applicable strategy from *The Art of War* is to know oneself and know your competitors. In the chapter on *guanxi* and negotiation we will address the importance Chinese companies attach to getting to know you through the *guanxi*-building process. You should make efforts to do the same, including the Chinese company's management, employees, suppliers, infrastructure, and market share. At the same time, you should also obtain more information about the business climate, such as the political, economic, social, technological strengths and weaknesses, public and media attitude towards your partner or competitor company. The more you know, the greater chance you will have of achieving your goals.

SUN ZI-LIKE STRATAGEMS AND CHINESE MENTALITY

Sun Zi's *The Art of War* has deeply influenced the social behaviors of the Chinese people for thousands of years and provided a key to understanding Chinese thinking and actions, both deliberate and inadvertent, in politics, military, and business. An anonymous writer in the late Ming Dynasty (1368–1644) or early Qing (1644–1911) period wrote *The Thirty-Six Stratagems* following Sun Zi's philosophy of winning without fighting but using a borrowed external force to deal with the opponent psychologically. This book has also exerted a great influence on the Chinese way of doing business. Researchers categorize these 36 stratagems into: stratagems of winning, stratagems of defending, stratagems of attacking, stratagems of scuffling, stratagems of merging, and stratagems of losing. We will discuss these in more detail in the chapters on negotiations. A selected list of *The Thirty-Six Stratagems* is included below:

- Kill with a borrowed knife
- Leisurely await the exhausted enemy
- Clamor in the east but attack in the west
- Create something out of nothing
- Hide a knife in a smile

- Beat the grass to startle the snake
- In order to capture, first let it go
- Remove the firewood from under the cooking pot
- Muddy the water to catch the fish
- Lure the enemy on to the roof, then take away the ladder

(Fang 1999, 166)

FYI

The popularity of *The Art of War* and *The Thirty-Six Stratagems* among Chinese is due largely to Chinese folk literature. *Romance of the Three Kingdoms* is acclaimed as a "textbook of Chinese stratagems developed from *The Art of War.*" It is so popular that almost everybody in Chinese-speaking communities, including illiterate people, knows about how the heroes in the novel use these stratagems to fight against enemies. Chinese children learn these stratagems through bed-time stories, TV dramas, and video games. These stratagems are also condensed into simple idioms that are easy to remember. It is no exaggeration to say that *The Art of War* and *The Thirty-Six Stratagems* are part of the Chinese blood that guide Chinese to cope with difficulties and opponents.

Sun Zi and the market place

Tracing the Roots of Chinese Business Culture

5

Having gained some knowledge of the impact of Confucianism on the everyday life of the Chinese people, you may be wondering how Chinese business culture has developed in a society that values spiritual cultivation and moral conduct but despises profit-related commercial activities. In this chapter we attempt to trace the roots of Chinese business culture within the Confucian tradition and the old bureaucratic system of Imperial China. We introduce two representative regional merchant groups in Chinese history and discuss the ways in which they did business. We focus on the connection between the basic approaches of these two groups and the primary principles of Confucianism regarding scholarship versus business, family and community, relationships with the government, and business ethics and reputation. Our goal is to help you associate the past with the present in order to better answer the question of how the Chinese do business.

EARLY COMMERCIAL DEVELOPMENT AND REGIONAL MERCHANT GROUPS

In the Chinese Confucian tradition, people doing business were located almost at the bottom of the social hierarchy. Scholars and government officials ranked highest as they had the responsibility to rule over the entire society. Next came the peasants who provided the necessities to feed and clothe people. The third rung was occupied by craftsmen and artisans. At the bottom of the hierarchy were the merchants, who did not produce anything substantial in the eyes of the people, but instead relied on the labor of others to make a living. Paradoxically, merchants generally made more money and had a better life than the majority of the population who farmed. The relatively easy money they earned from buying and selling made them look like cheaters and profiteers. One saying mirrors this general opinion: "*Wu shang bu jian*," literally "There's not a merchant who doesn't cheat." In Chinese there is no word for "businessman." The nearest equivalent, *shangren*, often has negative connotations.

Despite the low social status and negative image associated with people in trade, commerce developed through time in China, especially after the Southern Song Dynasty (1127–1279). One prominent phenomenon in the course of commercial development was the formation of regional merchant groups. Areas where natural conditions did not favor farming as a means of living generally produced a larger proportion of merchants. These merchants had to leave home and do something different. In the Ming Dynasty (1392–1644) and the Qing Dynasty (1644–1911), there were ten major regional merchant groups throughout the country. These early businessmen bought goods, such as tea and silk, at a low price from places where they were abundant, transported them far and wide using camels or boats, sold them to people in places where demand set a higher price, and earned profits as a reward.

From today's perspective, these merchants greatly promoted the country's commercial exchange, sped up economic development, and bettered the lives of the people at both ends of the buying and selling transaction. At the same time, they established a tradition for conducting business in this relationship-based and highly bureaucratic society. Looking at the historical development of these early merchants, we may find that in actual fact the Chinese business tradition complies with prevalent Confucian beliefs and principles of the times. This was despite the fact that businesses focus on making profits while Confucianism aims at educating people to restrain their personal desires and focus on building a well-ordered society. We illustrate this using two of the most representative and best-known merchant groups in Chinese history: *Jin Shang* (Shanxi Group) and *Hui Shang* (Huizhou Group). These two groups, one in the north and the other in the south, dominated Chinese commerce for hundreds of years until the mid-19th century when Western powers forced open the doors of China.

Shanxi Merchant Group (*Jin Shang*)

Historically, China was an agricultural society. However, Shanxi is an inland province situated on a plateau with little arable land, few water resources, and an arid climate. Shanxi also has a large population, four million in the early Ming Dynasty (1368–1644), equal to the populations of Hebei and Henan at that time. Unable to grow enough crops to feed so many, some Shanxi people had to seek other means of living. Fortunately, Shanxi had geographically strategic advantages as it bordered the northern section of the Great Wall, next to the nomads of Inner and Outer Mongolia. This enabled cross-border business, such as the bartering of horses, tea, fabric, and crops. In addition, the province had rich mineral resources and a developed handicraft industry, providing a substantial base for its merchants to start and expand their businesses.

Commercial activities in the province date back to the Qin Dynasty (221 BC–206 BC). In the Sui Dynasty (581–618) and the Tang Dynasty (618–907), a few commercial towns began to emerge, among them Zhangzhou and Datong. In the Tang Dynasty, Taiyuan became the northern capital, stimulating economic development in the surrounding areas. During the Song Dynasty (960–1279), Shanxi became an important trade hub and its merchants as a group began to gain a reputation. In the Yuan Dynasty (1271–1368), Shanxi merchants developed trade routes and organized camel caravans to transport goods far and wide. They purchased silk, sugar, fabric, and other goods from a variety of places and sold them as far away as Xinjiang and Mongolia. According to the travel log of Marco Polo (1254–1324), "Merchants originally from Taiyuan and Pingyang spread all over China, acquiring huge benefits." Taiyuan and Pingyang (now Linfen) are cities in Shanxi.

The rise of Shanxi merchants as an influential group occurred in the Ming Dynasty (1368–1644) when the government reformed the policy on the salt trade, a government monopoly and a highly profitable trade at that time. The new policy gave merchants the right to trade in salt if they could transport provisions to the borders for the army (Berliner 2003). Shanxi merchants took advantage of being closer to the borders and became major salt traders. The Shanxi group reached its peak in the Qing Dynasty by starting and expanding its money remittance business countrywide, making it China's top regional merchant group. According to the popular TV drama series *Qiao Family Courtyard*, of the total tax revenue collected by the Qing government from commercial and trading sectors throughout the country, roughly 30% was from Shanxi. Shanxi merchants led commercial advancement in China for about 500 years, from the Ming Dynasty until the Qing Dynasty. Their businesses covered tea, lumber, salt, and remittances. Salt trading and remittances were the most profitable, bringing the Shanxi group unmatched prosperity. By the mid-19th century, branches of Shanxi's remittance agencies could be found in most of China's major commercial cities and later in Japan and Korea. By the fall of the Qing Dynasty in 1911, Shanxi bankers practically monopolized the money transfer business throughout the country (Ma 2004). There was a saying in Beijing: "Most of the rich merchants in Beijing are Shanxi natives"

FYI

Remittance banks were called *piaohao* in Chinese. The first *piaohao* appeared in the early 19th century in Pingyao, a remote and little-known town in Shanxi. This was a revolutionary move in the development of commerce in the country. With a remittance service, merchants and long-distance travelers did not have to carry cash, which was usually in the form of silver coins. Instead, they used a draft issued by the bank to exchange for money at the designated branch wherever they traveled. This significantly benefited the Shanxi merchants who traveled far and wide for trade.

Huizhou Merchant Group (*Hui Shang*)

Huizhou consists of six counties and is located at the southern tip of Anhui Province among the hills and mountains with the well-known Mount Huangshan at its center. Like Shanxi, it has little arable land for people to grow crops. According to a Ming Dynasty gazetteer of one of its counties, only 7% of the land could be farmed. Huizhou, like Shanxi, had a large population. The shortage of land suitable for cultivation meant people were unable to make a living through farming. Instead they had to travel in order to trade local resources, such as tea and lumber, for rice from other locations. Fortunately they could use rivers to travel, including the Xin'an River that runs all the way to Hangzhou. This gave them an advantage to transport goods out of the mountains and bring back everyday necessities.

Most researchers believe that Huizhou merchants as a group came into being during the Southern Song Dynasty (1127–1279), when the nation's capital was relocated from Kaifeng of Henan to Lin'an (today's Hangzhou) to avoid the invading Jurchens. This relocation moved the nation's political center from the north to the south and stimulated the economic development of the area. One of the first business opportunities brought by this move was the building of the new capital, requiring a large amount of building materials. Huizhou happened to possess an abundance of timber, bamboo, and lacquer, and was only 200 kilometers away with easy river access. As a result, the Huizhou merchants made a fortune transporting and selling building materials for the new capital (Berliner 2003).

Huizhou, located between Zhejiang and Jiangsu, later became an important transportation and commercial hub. Its geographical position and river trading routes, like the Xin'an, meant that its people had ample opportunities to do trade. This resulted in a disproportionally large section of its population engaging in trade. Some records suggest that nine out of every ten families engaged in business. Young boys became apprentices at the age of 12 or 13, learning how to do business. By the age of 17, they had to leave home and do business wherever they could make money.

It is believed that the Huizhou group of merchants built up its power around the middle of the Ming Dynasty through trading in tea and timber, two main products of the area. They also began trading in salt from nearby sources after the government revised the salt-trading policy in 1492 (Berliner 2003). Huizhou merchants reached their peak during Qianlong's reign (1736–1796) when a number of Huizhou merchants turned to pawn-broking after the decline in the salt trade due to another new government policy. They opened pawnshops almost everywhere in the country, including Jiangsu in the north, Yunnan in the west, Fujian and Guangdong in the south, and even abroad in Japan and Thailand. "By the time of

---

FYI

Pawnshops are a type of financial enterprises that lend cash by holding collateral and charging interest. In the 18th century, pawnshops were important monetary resources in China where money-lending banks did not exist. The shops were for those who were in debt or in urgent need of cash. They went to pawnshops for cash loans, pledging household valuables as security. Once the contractual time elapsed, the pawnbroker could sell the pledged items at a price much higher than the amount of the loan. Pawn-broking was a capital-intensive but very profitable business sector.

Guanxu's reign (1875–1909), one could hardly find a pawnbroker not from Huizhou" (Berliner 2003).

Huizhou merchants dominated commerce in the southern part of China for about 300 years. They touched almost all profitable business sectors: tea, grain, silk, cloth, wood, paint, paper, ink, pottery, and so on. They also opened restaurants, hotels, and teahouses, as well as pawnshops. There was a saying that there was no town in which you could not find merchants from Huizhou (*"Wu hui bu cheng zhen"*).

TRADITIONAL BUSINESS CULTURE AND CONFUCIAN THOUGHTS

At this point you may be wondering how Shanxi and Huizhou merchants could succeed for so long in an anti-commercial culture. Over the past few years several TV drama series have been produced to depict these merchants, among them the already mentioned *Qiao Family Courtyard* (*Qiao Jia Dayuan*) and *Official Merchant Hu Xueyan* (*Hongding Shangren Hu Xueyan*). *Qiao Family Courtyard* records the development of a well-known Shanxi merchant, Qiao Zhiyong, who went from near bankruptcy to become one of the wealthiest men in China. *Official Merchant Hu Xueyan* tells the story of a legendary Huizhou merchant. The dramas present the hardships of early Shanxi and Huizhou merchants, the ways in which they won the trust of their customers, the principles to follow in doing business, and their attempts to build a relationship with the government.

Scholars from different disciplines have tried to trace the path of these two groups and explain how they started, succeeded, and declined. Based on their research, we can argue that the success of *Jin Shang* and *Hui Shang* was due partly to their diligence, endurance, entrepreneurship, and business acumen. These same traits can be found in almost all successful businessmen in the world. Geographical conditions and historical incidences also played a crucial role in their success. However, there are other factors that made them stand out. In the following, we will compare and contrast the business culture these early-day merchants established and the basic Confucian principles that have influenced the Chinese for about two thousand years. Our focus will be on attitudes towards business versus scholarship, family and community values, business reputation (face), role of the government, and importance of moral cultivation and self-disciplines.

Attitudes towards Confucian Scholarship and Business Pursuits

The famous Confucian saying *"Xiaoren zhong yu li, Junzi yu yu yi"* aptly sums up the attitude that profit-driven merchants were despised while gentlemen *(junzi)*, another name of Confucian scholars, were held in high esteem. In the first part of the saying, *xiaoren* literally means "small-men" or narrow-minded and self-centered men. In the second part which means "gentlemen value virtue and commitment," the word *yi* is used to describe important Confucian principles pertaining to one's duty to family, friends, community, and country. As discussed in Chapter 3, talented young men in ancient China shared one ultimate goal (*"Xue er you ze shi"*): to study Confucian classics, practice writing pre-styled expository articles, pass the imperial civil service exams, and become a government official. If someone succeeded, he would be highly respected as an exemplary figure for the people in the surrounding area and his family would rise in prestige and wealth. Only those who could neither study nor farm went into business. Elevating the social status of scholarship and downgrading business practice (*"Zhong ru qing shang"*) was the dominant belief in Chinese culture for thousands of years. However, Shanxi and Huizhou merchants held somewhat different attitudes.

People in Shanxi believed that there was nothing wrong with learning to do business. Excelling in business was not at all inferior to excelling in scholarship. These two should not be contradictory but interrelated. To do business well, people need to be knowledgeable about the market, wise in deciding when to buy and sell, unafraid of hardships when traveling far, and skillful in maintaining good relationships with people, including customers and government. Growing up in such a social atmosphere, many talented young men in the province chose to give up the long and competitive study-scholar-bureaucrat path, taking instead the study-merchant path. With the latter, they could quickly achieve monetary success, which was more substantial and time efficient.

Huizhou, however, differed from the overall tradition and Shanxi's attitude towards scholarship and business pursuits. It valued both scholarship and business, (*"Rui gu bing Zhong"*), although to varying degrees. As mentioned in the previous section, almost every family in Huizhou was doing business in order to survive in a place inhospitable to agriculture, so there was no reason to look down upon people in trade. But deep down they still valued scholarship more than business practice, which was just a means for making a living.

Huizhou was the hometown of Zhu Xi (1130–1200), the most influential neo-Confucian philosopher in Chinese history. Under the influence of his thoughts, people in Huizhou considered education the most important thing in life—if they were already able to feed and clothe themselves. With the wealth gained from business, Huizhou merchants built schools in their hometowns to prepare their juniors for the imperial examinations. Even young boys from poor families could receive an education with money from their rich relatives. Huizhou merchants also built lodging houses in large cities for the Huizhou examinees to study and prepare for the examinations. Records show that in the Ming and Qing dynasties (966–1911), more than 2,000 Huizhou natives passed the highest level of imperial examinations and were granted the title of *Jinshi*. So Huizhou was not only well known for its successful merchant group, but also as a place that cultivated a disproportionally larger number of scholars and government officials.

FYI

There are many other things that have contributed to Huizhou's scholarly tradition. It is known for its high-quality writing brushes, ink-sticks, paper, and ink stones (*wen fang si bao*). In the Song and Tang dynasties, Huizhou was a center for engraving books. This allowed records of Huizhou culture to be maintained, including private contracts, land deeds, genealogies, travel logs, and account books. In addition, Huizhou merchants built gardens, temples, museums, archways, and bridges using the wealth gained from business. These have become a valuable source for scholars today, from both West and East, to study and understand Chinese culture, resulting in a new academic discipline *Huixue* or Huizhou Studies.

Scholarly Businessmen (*Ru-Shang*)

In traditional Chinese culture, scholars and merchants were positioned almost at opposite ends of the social hierarchy. However, these two ends can be linked together and combined into a new category entitled "*Ru-Shang*," or Confucian businessmen or scholar-businessmen. This term refers to the kind of business people who are knowledgeable about Confucianism and do business following general Confucian principles.

Huizhou merchants were considered prominent examples of such scholarly merchants, as illustrated by an ancient saying, "*Hui Shang duo Ru*

Shang," meaning "Many of Huizhou merchants are scholar-businessmen." It was said that many Huizhou merchants did business during the day but read Confucian classics, composed poems, and drew paintings in the evening. Whenever they met they discussed scholarly topics, such as how to interpret a difficult sentence from a literary piece, and spent money on building gardens, academies, and libraries. In actual fact, many Huizhou businessmen were also well-known scholars.

The passion for studying Confucius in Huizhou or among Huizhou natives greatly enhanced the image of Huizhou merchants as a group and changed people's old perception of businessmen who only knew profits. For example, Cheng Dawei (1533–1606), a Huizhou merchant in the Ming Dynasty, was known for his contribution to the better use of the abacus. His business experience enabled him to set up the standard format for the abacus and perfect its calculation rhythms. His theories soon spread to other places, including Japan and Korea, giving Huizhou merchants another edge in the development of commerce in China. Written records provide more examples. *The Huizhou Chronicle of the Jiaqing Era* (1796–1821) describes Huizhou merchants as "properly dressed, well-spoken like scholars," "fully aware of prices, knowing when to buy and sell, and gaining extra profits from selling local goods at other places."

Shanxi merchants did not have the reputation for scholarly cultivation as Huizhou merchants, however this did not mean that people in Shanxi disdained scholarship. They also encouraged their juniors to study hard, although the goal might not necessarily be to take exams and obtain a government position. To many of them, the purpose of learning was to do well in business, which meant that successful Shanxi merchants were well educated. Historical records show that some Shanxi examinees who had passed the imperial examinations chose to take over the family business instead of accepting the official titles (Berliner 2003, 7). The hero of *Qiao Family Courtyard* was a typical scholarly merchant. He had to quit the imperial examination to take over the family business because of a family tragedy. He was knowledgeable, articulate, and had extraordinary business acumen, all of which contributed to his success in business.

The image of *Ru-Shang* or scholarly businessmen, helped these people win trust and respect from customers and government officials. To the customers, they were not just greedy profit-seekers but men who applied Confucian principles to guide and discipline their business conduct. To government officials, these *Ru-Shang* were gentlemen with whom they could be friends.

In China today, the best unofficial title granted to people in industry and commerce is *Ru-Shang*. The press has used the title of *Ru-Shang* to refer to the CEO of the Haier Group, China's leading electronics manufacturer. He loves reading books, ranging from Chinese classics to newly published works on Western management.

Official Businessmen (*Guan Shang*)

Imperial China had no fixed rules or standards for the legal structure of government bureaucracy. The government functioned as policy-makers, administrators, tax collectors, and legal arbiters, playing a decisive role in business operation and expansion. One had to master Confucian classics and pass the imperial examinations in order to qualify as a member of the ruling class. In theory, government officials had to maintain a high level of integrity and discipline by following the Confucian code of moral conduct. However, in practice this was not always the case. Either way, businesses of the time had to deal with government officials and it goes without saying that it was important to establish a sound relationship with the government officials on all levels in order to gain privilege, or at least not to lose a war of interest against other merchants.

As mentioned earlier, through the imperial examination system, the most talented people were selected to take official government posts. This was especially true in the Ming and Qing dynasties when most government officials were scholars. It was therefore easier for Huizhou *Ru-Shang* to network with scholar-officials. Indeed, the government also needed the support of the merchants, who were important taxpayers and could donate their wealth when the government was in need. For example, Huizhou merchants built exquisite gardens to welcome Emperor Qianlong during his six tours to the southern part of China, spending a fortune hosting him and his entourage. These efforts translated into many business advantages and opportunities. Huizhou merchants also invested a lot of money building study rooms for their juniors, hiring good teachers, and sending more people to take the imperial examinations. After the successful examinees became government officials, they could influence the imperial bureaucracy, gaining more commercial advantages for Huizhou merchants, such as the long-held salt trading monopoly in southern China.

In the Qing Dynasty, money could buy official positions. Some wealthy merchants simply bought themselves a position and became a *Guan-Shang* (official-merchant). In Shanxi, the purpose of study was to do well in business. Money earned from business could then be used to buy a position in the government. This was the so-called scholar-businessman-bureaucrat path (*"Xue er you ze gu, gu er you ze shi"*), shorter and more effective than the scholar-bureaucrat path. Many wealthy Shanxi businessmen or their sons used money to buy a post. The third son of the Qiao family became an official this way. By doing so, these merchants gained fame and glory as well as more business opportunities to earn more wealth. Another example was the Wang family, one of the four wealthiest families in Shanxi, who spent a great deal of money bribing officials, helping the family become a greater player in the salt trade. The Shanxi bankers' role as the official Qing remittance agents was also the result of a close relationship between the government and merchants. This type of under-the-counter relationship benefited both officials and merchants.

However, every coin has two sides. The collaboration or conspiracy between businesses and government might bring these businessmen some advantages. Nevertheless, if a particular official left his post or if the government policy changed, then business could be jeopardized. When the Qing government announced the liberalization of the salt trade in order to collect more tax and avoid salt smuggling, a large number of salt merchants in both groups lost their monopoly privileges. Some went bankrupt while others had to turn to other businesses. The same happened with the tea trade in the late Qing Dynasty when the government had to open up the country to foreign trade. The decline of both the Huizhou merchants and the Shanxi merchants was in a way directly related to the wane of the Qing Dynasty.

Establishing and maintaining good relationships with local and central governments was and still is a tradition in China. Throughout this book, we have alerted you again and again to the importance of establishing a good relationship or *guanxi* while doing business in China. We do not encourage you to bribe government officials, which is illegal both in China and in your home country, however, we hope you will build a healthy relationship by means that are beneficial to you, government, customers, and society as a whole.

Family, Community, and Business Partnership

In Imperial China, there were no well-defined laws and regulations to guide and restrain people's behavior. This was the cause as well as the effect of Confucius's emphasis on family and community, as we discussed in Chapter 3. A strong social order and long-term relationship within any type of community were what people relied upon to gain support in times of difficulties, secure property, and honor verbal and written contracts. Traditional Chinese businesses were primarily family based and community supported. Shanxi and Huizhou merchants were no exceptions.

They relied on their own communities to hire employees, collect capital to expand business, obtain business information, work together to avoid internal competition, and compete against merchants from other places, not to mention seek support from government officials from the same area.

According to Huang (1996), Shanxi remittance banks only hired people who were natives of Shanxi. The apprentices recruited had to go through careful background checks and required third-party guarantors. If any staff member was caught and dismissed for cheating, that person would never find another position in any other Shanxi bank. In businesses run by Huizhou merchants, the main staff members, including managers, accountants, and sales agents, had to be family members, members of the same lineage, or members of their domestic staff. In other words, they did not trust people from outside their network. This traditional hiring mechanism was one of the contributing factors to the long-lasting growth and dominance of the two merchant groups in Chinese commercial history.

At that time, family and community were almost the only sources of capital for expanding business in China, as there were no banks from which to borrow money. Long-term trust was the key. Qiao Zhiyong, the hero of the TV drama series *Qiao Family Courtyard*, collected the capital he needed from his neighbors for a tea-trading trip from the south to the north. Community was also a place to coordinate business in order to avoid internal competition. Records show that each of the Huizhou merchants had his own territory for business. If another Huizhou merchant planned to do the same business, he had to start his business outside that territory.

Both merchant groups were known for their internal support in times of need and difficulty. Shanxi merchants organized a large business network for mutual support and cooperation in order to strengthen their power as a group. Likewise, among different Huizhou communities, commercial networks were set up to share information, channel business opportunities, and establish partnership collaborations. For example, the 500 tightly united Huizhou merchant pawnshops in Nanjing successfully drove out Fujian merchants with a below-market interest rate. In Yangzhou, Huizhou merchants took away the dominant market share of the Shanxi group in salt trading (Ma 2004).

Business Ethics, Reputations, and Rules

The goal of business people is to make profits, but the "how" is what differentiates them. It is hard to discern a cause-and-effect connection between a high percentage of ethical merchants within these two merchant groups and their long-time dominance of Chinese trade and commerce. However, stories do exist about Confucian-inspired deeds performed by businessmen from both groups.

One such story is about a Huizhou merchant in the Ming Dynasty who sold grain in a disaster year at a price that was no higher than in a normal year. When people asked him why he did this, he said that he made money from his customers. If they could survive the disaster, he would make more money in the future. Another story is about an ink merchant from Huizhou who found that the ink he had purchased was of bad quality. He immediately bought back all the ink he had sold at a higher price and destroyed the remainder of his stock. Similar stories can be found among Shanxi merchants. In a severe three-year drought, one of the biggest Shanxi merchant families offered free food to hungry people and saved many lives. To this family, winning the trust of current and potential customers and building a good reputation were more important than earning temporary profits. Face is important to the Chinese; some people consider it second only to life. Face in business is as important as the brand or store name a business possesses. What the businessmen did in the above stories was to build a good reputation and win trust and respect from their customers. It was not only beneficial to the customer and society, but also to their long-term business.

As mentioned above, Confucianism values harmony among people in the family, work place, and society. This harmony is achieved not through rules or financial merit but through human goodness, moral cultivation, and restraining the desire for more. One historical figure who lived 2,000 years ago bound the Shanxi merchants together in moral strength. Guan Yu, a native of Shanxi, was renowned for his loyalty and honesty. The people of Shanxi province are proud of and revere him, even building temples in memory of him in many cities of China where Shanxi merchants gathered.

Huizhou merchants were bound together by Confucian beliefs. We discussed earlier that Huizhou people valued education and even children from poor families could go to school. This in a way enabled people there to grow up with the Confucian code of conduct which they applied both in daily life and in business.

In later years, some modern corporate concepts were introduced into the traditional businesses operated by Huizhou and Shanxi merchants. For example, Shanxi remittance banks hired managers who had a clean background check but who were not directly related to the bank owners, although they still had to be Shanxi natives. They also set up a reward system by giving dividends to staff members so they would care more about the long-term interest of the store (Ma 2004). Huizhou pawnshops generally held a lot of valuable goods, due to the nature of the business. One Huizhou merchant wrote a book for young people on how to enter the trade entitled *Essential Information for Pawnshop Operation*. In the book, he clearly stated that people in the trade should be upright and diligent. They should be careful when making friends and should not smoke opium and be lazy (Berliner 2004).

Associate the Past with the Present

The fortunes of both groups declined when Western powers came to China. They have never regained their past glories. Many of their descendants now reside in large cities, such as Shanghai, Beijing, and Tianjin. They seldom think about the golden days of their ancestors.

Needless to say, not all of the Shanxi and Huizhou merchants were ethical and honest. However, it is important for us to highlight the tradition upon which Chinese business culture was established. This tradition is primarily derived from Confucian thoughts regarding family, community, governmental hierarchy, integrity, education, and personal efforts.

In modern-day China, the market economy has virtually replaced the old planned economy and businessmen are no longer at the bottom of society. Instead, they are synonymous with success and wealth, although some are still associated with such negative words as "dishonesty" and "cheating." But tradition is tradition and it is hard to remove all traces of the past.

6 Regional Differences in Business Culture

A s you have already read in previous chapters, the Confucian cultural tradition has dominated China for about two thousand years. Despite being repressed during the Mao era, its principles have influenced the way most Chinese view the world, as well as their attitudes towards family, outsiders, authority, and social recognition. However, China is so vast in size that within this fundamental tradition some variations can be found from region to region. These variations are mainly due to geographic locations, political status, and the way people of an area have made their living over generations. These in turn influence the way people of a region conduct business with each other and with outsiders. In this chapter we shift our focus to regional business cultures by introducing three of China's most representative regions.

GENERAL REGIONAL STEREOTYPES

There is an old Chinese saying: "Every place raises its own people" ("*Yi fang shuitu yang yi fang ren*"). It implies that people from a certain place possess a particular set of common traits that are not found in people from other places. Because of this, the Chinese love to identify their

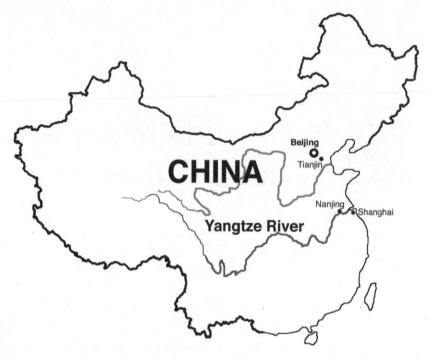

China: north and south divided by the Yangtze River

geographic selves. For example, when two Chinese meet for the first time, one of the first questions asked is, "Where are you from?" The answer provides an initial impression of a person, even to the point of influencing a potential business relationship. During future interactions each party will continue to observe and judge if the other person possesses the perceived common features of people from that particular region. At some point one party may tell the other whether he or she is typical of the people from their place of origin.

Broadly speaking, the Chinese are grouped into northerners and southerners. The Yangtze River is generally believed to be the dividing line between north and south but this boundary is not clear-cut at all. For example, to the people in places like Beijing and Shandong in the north, those from south of the Yangtze River are southerners. However, in the eyes of the Cantonese, Shanghai is too far north to be grouped with them as southerners.

It is generally thought that the northern Chinese are relatively tall, loud, frank, warm-hearted, loyal to each other, and conservative. Southerners are perceived as shorter, softer spoken, smarter, more hardworking, adventurous, calculating, and wealthy. Of course, these are rough stereotypes and there are many exceptions and deviations. Even so, given that they may be true, they can be further differentiated into provinces, cities, or even smaller regional units. In addition, stereotypical regional characteristics have become blurred and watered down due to urbanization and migration as a result of social and economic reforms. Despite this, regional traits can still be identified in people from a particular place, one reason why the Chinese remain interested in learning what region someone comes from.

China is so large that it would be impossible to give details of every region. We have therefore chosen three of the most representative regions and summarized their history, geographical conditions, stereotypical traits, and suggestions for our readers. These three regions are: the Beijing–Tianjin area; the Yangtze River Delta; and the Zhujiang (Pearl) River Delta. We chose these three because they are the most developed and wealthiest regions with the largest consumer markets in the country. We assume that they are the places most likely for you to either have existing business options or consider for potential opportunities.

BEIJING–TIANJIN AREA

The Beijing–Tianjin area is located in the northeastern part of China close to the birthplace of Confucius and the cradle of Chinese civilization. Under the influence of Confucian philosophy, people in this area are generally traditional and conservative by nature. They value face and care how others view them. They follow closely social formalities, such as using the polite form of the word "you" (*nin* instead of *ni*) to people who are older and/or of higher social status. They value experience and authority and prefer to use official or professional titles to address people, even in non-work settings. *Guanxi* is a catchword to them. They are proud to have an extensive network and know important people, and they love to share such information with others. They love to establish and maintain friendship-like, long-term business relationships. They are warmhearted, outspoken, and open armed to friends and people they trust. At the dinner table, they order the best dishes for their guests, urge them to eat and drink, and struggle to pay for the meal.

In return they expect their friends, guests, associates to treat them in the same way and be honest, helpful, loyal, and respectful. So before your business trip, please read this book carefully and follow our advice closely.

Beijing and Tianjin on the map of China

For example, try to respect experience and authority, use the proper form of address, and work to establish *guanxi* or network. Show them your title if it is an impressive one, tell them if your company is a big name in the industry, and share with them any success stories of your company in the domestic and international markets. If you need help or have little idea about how to deal with a certain situation, be honest and ask for their help and suggestions.

Beijing

Beijing has been China's capital for hundreds of years, except for some short periods. Beijing is synonymous with the People's Republic of China for people in China and abroad. Beijing people or Beijingers are very proud of their geographic identity. For the past few decades, since the founding of the People's Republic of China, the government has invested heavily in building the city and turning it into the political, cultural, commercial, academic, transportation, and industrial center of the country. Not surprisingly Beijing has the best of almost everything, including the best universities, busiest railway hub, largest airport, and most authoritative TV station, not to mention the Great Wall and Forbidden City. Because of its prominent position in China, Beijing has attracted leading multinational companies and banks to set up regional headquarters or branches. Foreign companies always choose Beijing to establish their business presence in China before expanding to other areas. Good examples include MacDonald's and Starbucks. For most overseas returnees and college graduates, Beijing is always their first choice to develop careers on their return or upon graduation.

Although they share many of the traditional characteristics found in most northern Chinese, Beijing people exhibit some special features not usually found in non-Beijingers. For example, living in a city of superlatives, Beijing people possess an inborn sense of pride and superiority, at least in the eyes of people from other places. They are eloquent and articulate, very different from the traditional image of the Chinese being quiet and reserved. The first time you visit Beijing you may experience their eloquence as soon as you leave the airport. Your taxi driver may find a means to start a conversation with you if you happen to speak some Chinese. By the time you arrive at your destination, you may already know a lot about his income and family while at the same time having told him which country you are from, if you have a family, and why you are visiting Beijing. You may also feel pleased about his compliments on your Chinese proficiency and be grateful for his suggestions and advice for living and working in the city.

Living close to the central government, people in Beijing seem to have some element of political zeal. They can talk at length about Iraq prisoner abuse, Taiwan elections, Hillary Clinton and Barrack Obama, government interference in the stock market, and the 2008 Beijing Olympic Games. You may be surprised when a taxi driver eloquently and confidently tells you why a certain government leader has disappeared from the TV screen for the past few days or when a female blue-collar worker makes a thorough analysis of the pros and cons of Bush's policy on Iraq. There is a joke about this Beijing characteristic: a random passer-by in the Beijing streets knows more about politics than many politicians outside Beijing.

The eloquence and broad knowledge of Beijing people may give you an easier and more relaxing time when you do business there or with Beijing natives. Finding a topic to strike up a conversation can often come easily. At the negotiation table, their eloquence can easily lighten an atmosphere that would otherwise be too serious and formal. Here we would like to suggest that before your trip you should give an eye to what has happened

An eloquent Beijinger

in the world so that you can find some common ground with your Beijing business partners. Your knowledge and intellectual conversation can help you gain the respect and liking of your Chinese counterparts. Such casual conversations can also narrow the psychological and ideological distance between you and them, making your job much easier. Nevertheless, friendly and expressive as they are, Beijing people are very patriotic and sensitive about certain topics. You should be careful about your attitude and wording when you touch upon topics like human rights and the trade wars between the US and China.

Beijing attracts a high-quality talent pool. Businessmen in the city are generally well educated and cultured. Some of them can read, write, and speak English and are able to speak about business without using a translator. They like to invite you to upscale restaurants and top-notch coffee houses. Their conversation topics may include golfing, vacations in Sweden, or even the prices of private airplanes.

Perhaps because Beijing is the political center of the country, its business people value power and network more than people from anywhere else in China. They know how power can give access to inside information that is key to business success, and how networks with the government can channel business opportunities that are otherwise hard to obtain. In Beijing there are many government-sponsored companies or firms run by the sons and daughters of current, retired, or late high-ranking officials. *Guan Shang* (official-businessmen) is the term often used to categorize them. Businesses with no direct connections have to use other means to obtain inside information or rely on their own observation and analysis. Therefore, you may sometimes find that Beijing businessmen are sensitive to political ups and downs and tend to overlook the pitfalls or potential of the market. But if you decide to do business with them, you have to accept their ways. In choosing a partner in Beijing, you should try to find a government-related company or rely on local people to help find you one. It will save you a lot of time and effort and almost certainly guarantee your business success. Of course there are two sides to the coin: the government official related to your Beijing business partner may one day leave his post. To maintain your business standing there and protect your own interests you should try to develop your own network so that you can move on with new partners should the need arise.

Tianjin

Tianjin is about 100 kilometers from Beijing and for a long time has lived in the shadow of the capital, despite a long tradition of commerce and industry dating back to the middle of the 19th century. Tianjin's proximity to Beijing prevented its full development, even though it is one of the four municipalities directly under the central government and the third-largest city in the country. In recent years, the central government has decided to develop Tianjin, especially the Tianjin Economic-Technological Development Area (TEDA) located 130 kilometers from Beijing. Tianjin boasts one of the largest seaports functioning as an import and export hub for the northern part of the country, making it essential for Beijing's own development.

Tianjin is a good choice if you want to do business in northern China because of its relatively low cost of living, cheap labor, proximity to the capital, well-developed commerce and industry, excellent highway network, convenient access to the seaport, and less competitive market. You may receive more attention and government support there, since most foreign businesses head to Beijing and tend to ignore this city. Although so close to Beijing, people in Tianjin seem more Chinese than people in the capital. They also like to talk, but they prefer topics that are more relaxing and closer to everyday life. Tianjin business people, although not as sophisticated and cultured as their counterparts in Beijing, are more practical and down to earth.

YANGTZE RIVER DELTA

The Yangtze River Delta refers to the areas covering Shanghai, Zhejiang, and Jiangsu with Shanghai in the middle. In geographic terms, it is perhaps the best location in China. It has a mild climate, rich water resources, and fertile land. All these offer its people advantageous conditions for agriculture and commercial activities. However, this area is densely populated with too many people yet too little arable land. People from this region have traditionally left home to make a living in other locations. However, since the start of the economic reforms in the late 1970s, the area has developed rapidly and become the wealthiest region in China. According to the US–China Business Council, this area accounts for a quarter of China's GDP, nearly half of the total foreign direct investment in China, and more than one-third of the country's total volume of foreign trade. Table 6.1 shows the region's economic contribution to China as a whole.

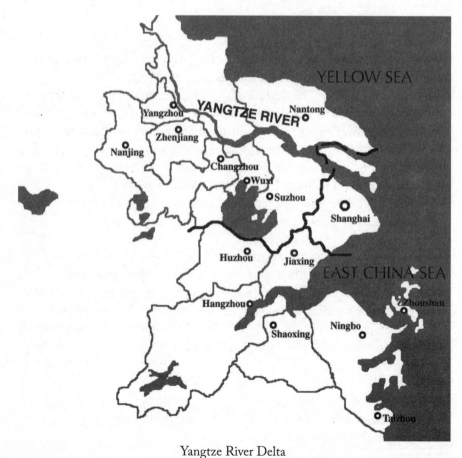

Yangtze River Delta

Table 6.1 Yangtze River Delta (YRD) as % of China's total, first half of 2005

Population (2004)	10.1%
GDP	25.6%
Imports	35.5%
Exports	38.8%
Contracted FDI	43.3%
Utilized FDI	52.1%

Source: China National Bureau of Statistics

As already mentioned in the previous chapter, during the Southern Song Dynasty, the national capital was moved to Hangzhou, the provincial capital of Zhejiang. This move brought a large number of migrants from the Central Plains, which was deeply rooted in the culture of Confucianism. As a result, the new capital area has developed a unique culture with a strong Confucian influence, for example, emphasizing experience and viewing things as a whole. But compared to people in the north, people in this region are gentler, more implicit, reticent, practical, and hard working. They are committed to seeking a better life through their own hands and brainpower. We have selected Shanghai and Wenzhou for further discussion.

Shanghai

Although Beijing is the country's capital, in many ways Shanghai is China's number-one city. It is the largest city in population as well as the most developed city in mainland China with the highest standard of living and highest GDP. Shanghai also has several world number ones. As of December 2005, Shanghai Port is the largest and busiest in the world. Donghai Bridge is the world's longest cross-sea bridge at 32.5 kilometers. In 2002, German Transrapid constructed in Shanghai the first commercial Maglev railway. When you enter the city, you will be amazed at the exotic flavor of Shanghai's city center and the magnificent metropolitan skyline of the Lujiazui area, where you will find branches of the world's leading banks and insurance companies. You can find all the top brands, upmarket restaurants, and many luxurious hotels. Some people assert that Shanghai has the potential to replace Hong Kong as the center of finance in Asia. Shanghai is a symbol of the new economic reform and the new China, an engine of the country's economic development, and the country's financial and economic center.

The skyline of Pudong in Shanghai
(Reprinted with permission from INMAGINE)

Shanghai has geographical advantages. Unlike Beijing, which is surrounded by mountains and plains, Shanghai is situated in the middle of China's eastern coastline, at the mouth of the country's water highway, the Yangtze River. The Huangpu and Wusong Rivers also flow through Shanghai. All of these elements contributed to its rapid development, beginning in the 19th century as a trade hub with the West when the foreign invasion forced open the doors of China. From then until the 20th century, Shanghai witnessed waves of foreign settlements including British, American, French, and Russian. In the first half of the 20th century, Shanghai became the cultural and economic center of Asia and was known as the "Paradise of Adventurers" and "Paris of the East." It was the birthplace of many things that led to modern China, including China's first motor car driven on a road, first train tracks, and the Chinese film industry.

Shanghai boasts a unique culture, which is called *haipai*, or Shanghai style. It is a combination of Western and Chinese culture. If you do business in Shanghai, you may find that people there are more open-minded and willing to embrace new things. They are more likely to follow international norms and honor legal documents, such as contracts. They are willing to enter into a business relationship with outsiders in the short term provided money can be made. They seldom mix personal feelings with business and know how to obtain and protect personal rights and interests. Unlike Beijingers, they value benefits more than fame and power and are more sensitive to market trends rather than political atmosphere. Business is business in Shanghai, more so than in Beijing and many other places in China.

Nevertheless, you may prefer Beijing's style as Shanghai business people are sometimes too clever, careful, calculating, and particular about details. At the negotiation table, you may have to be very patient since they may spend a long time over details and need to be fully convinced before making a business decision. On top of that, they may appear arrogant because you are just one of their choices, a characteristic shared by many Shanghai people. In their eyes, people from other places are not smart enough and grabbing their business is something impractical. Shanghai and Beijing are both rather sensitive about each other as their only rival in the country: both want to be the country's number one. In different ways and from different perspectives both cities are number one, to outsiders at least.

Wenzhou

Compared to Beijing, Tianjin, and Shanghai, Wenzhou is a medium-sized city situated in the southeastern province of Zhejiang, 500 kilometers south of Shanghai. Surrounded by mountains and open seas, Wenzhou has a large population but limited resources and poor transportation. For these reasons, during the Mao era, the central government ignored it and did not build any large state-owned enterprises as they did in Beijing, Tianjin, and Shanghai. Historically, Wenzhou functioned as a seaport connecting the interior mountainous southern area of Zhejiang with the outside world. In 1876, it opened to the foreign tea trade, although there were no Western settlements, probably because of its location. It became an important port during the Second Sino–Japanese War (1937–1945) since it was one of the few ports still under Chinese control. Wenzhou is also known for its emigrants to Europe and the United States who opened restaurants and other small businesses. There are reportedly 400,000 Wenzhou natives residing in over 100 countries and regions. These overseas connections have made the Wenzhou people more open-minded, enterprising, and less conservative than most Chinese under the influence of traditional Confucian beliefs.

Unlike the big-name cities, such as Beijing and Shanghai, Wenzhou did not receive much special support from the central government during the economic reforms in terms of finance and policies. However, in the more liberal atmosphere brought about by the reforms, Wenzhou has become well-known throughout the country for its well-developed individual and rural businesses, its low costs, low-end commodities, such as buttons, lighters, and shoes, and its countrywide diaspora.

Many economists and researchers of other disciplines are interested in the Wenzhou phenomenon or "Wenzhou Model." They conclude that Wenzhou people work extremely hard with what they have or rather with what they lack. They are willing to leave home and settle down in any place where they can find a means of earning a living. They have an outstanding business sense and can always find the opportunities others overlook. Compared to business people in Beijing and Shanghai, people in Wenzhou are not well educated and are therefore less sophisticated and more down to earth. Because of this, they don't care so much about face, as most Chinese do. Instead, they are known to have a "thick" face and can do things that most urban Chinese despise, such as running barber-shops, repairing shoes, and fixing windows. They like to be their own boss and dare to take risks. In recent years, many Wenzhou people have set their sights on the housing markets using capital earned from other

Wenzhou speculators boosted China's house prices

businesses. In Shanghai alone, they spent RMB 3 billion in one year on house purchases. Their incursion into the housing market has contributed to the rocketing house prices across the country.

If you have an opportunity to do business with Wenzhou natives or, more broadly speaking, people from the Yangtze River Delta (excluding Shanghai), you will soon find you are working with a group of enterprising, intelligent, and down-to-earth people who are different from the more conservative and slow-paced northern Chinese. The southerners are more independent, self reliant, and market oriented with sophisticated social skills. At the negotiation table, for example, they tend to say little but listen attentively. From bits and pieces based on what the other side says, they can quickly take stock of the other party and decide on their next move. This tactic may make you recall Sun Zi's famous quotation: "Know yourself and know your counterpart (enemy), you will win always." With all their rich experience dealing with people from different regions, they excel at adjusting their tactics to suit the social status, position, purpose, and perspectives of their opposite number. You may say that they are too cunning, but it is this very social skill that helps them settle down all over the country and merge well with the local people.

PEARL RIVER DELTA

Beijing and Shanghai are definitely the best-known places in China. However, Guangzhou and Shenzhen, two of the best-developed cities in the Pearl River Delta, are by no means inferior in status and fame. The Pearl River Delta is located in the south of Guangdong Province. Because of its proximity to Hong Kong, among other advantages, it was chosen to test the market-oriented economy in the socialist context at the initial stage of the economic reform launched in 1978 by Deng Xiaoping. Over the past three decades, large amounts of foreign investment have flooded into the area with which a large number of joint-venture and foreign-owned factories have been set up. These factories produce a great quantity of made-in-China goods that are exported to global markets. In 2001, this area provided about 5% of the world's goods and contributed over 8% of the nation's economy, although it occupies only 0.4% of China's total area. The rapid development of the Beijing–Tianjin area and the Yangtze River Delta in recent years has resulted in something of a status demotion for the Pearl River Delta, once the wealthiest and most

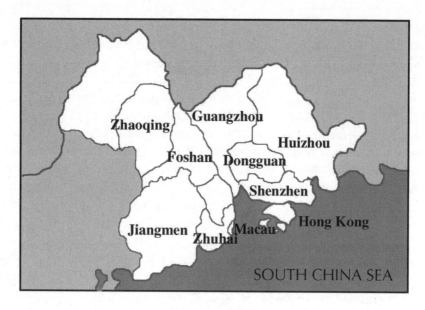

Pearl River Delta

economically dynamic area of China, yet it is still an ideal place to start and do business in China.

In ancient China, Guangzhou (Canton), where the delta is located, was a foreign land to the people in the north since people there looked different, spoke a different dialect, and worshipped different gods and goddesses. Being distant from the center of the Chinese civilization in the north, this area did not receive much influence from China's mainstream philosophy deeply rooted in Confucianism. They have never looked down upon business people as the people in the north did. Instead, many people in the area traveled overseas to seek a better life in foreign countries. They started small businesses in their adopted homes and built up the numerous Chinatowns all over the world.

With more contacts with the outside world, business people in the Pearl River Delta area are more open to new ideas and willing to work with outsiders. In practice, they are not afraid to take risks and can quickly sense and seize new opportunities. To them, business is business and business is to make profits. Efficiency, quantity, and quality are their first concern rather than political games and relationships. They are low-key people and don't like to talk much. Nevertheless, they also value face like northerners, but in a different way. They love to use branded products, including clothes, cars, and watches, and wear large gold rings, a clear indication to their business partners and clients that they have sufficient capital and economic strength. Probably because of their long-standing fear of Mother Nature threatening the safety of their traditional fishermen in the ocean, people in the area are very superstitious and have a lot of taboos. They believe in fengshui, fate, face, and palm reading. They place images of deities in their stores, homes, and offices. They believe in lucky numbers, lucky dates, and lucky colors. They always look up the calendar to check if a certain day and time are good for the things they plan to do, for example, open a store or sign a business contract. So if you do business with Guangdong natives, please be very careful. You'd better consult the local people or business partner as to when, where, and how. For your convenience, we also provide some relevant information in the last chapter of the book.

Guangzhou and Shenzhen, although very different from each other, are exemplary representatives in the region.

Guangzhou

Guangzhou, formerly known in the West as Canton, is 120 kilometers northwest of Hong Kong. It is the provincial capital of Guangdong and the most important city in southern China. For a long time, even before the economic reforms, Guangzhou was famous for its Canton Trade Fair held every spring and autumn. The fair started in 1957 when China's doors were closed to the outside world. Back then, it was almost the only window for Chinese businesses to catch a glimpse of the outside world and a platform to do business with foreign companies. At present, the Canton Trade Fair is still the largest in the nation, attracting hundreds of Chinese and foreign companies. Since the commodities displayed and sold in the fair are of high quality, it is an ideal place for you to choose Chinese products to export to your country and/or to locate a suitable Chinese business partner.

Guangzhou has a long history in commerce and shipping. The first Europeans, the Portuguese, arrived here about 500 years ago. In 1683, when China claimed control of Taiwan and encouraged foreign trade, Guangzhou was the only official trade port until more treaty ports were opened in the 1840s. In the 1980s and early 1990s, Guangzhou took the lead in developing the market economy, becoming the national icon of opening-up and economic reforms.

Shenzhen

Shenzhen was a fishing village before China initiated its open-door policy and economic reforms. It was singled out in the late 1970s because of its proximity to Hong Kong to pilot the bold project of setting up Special Economic Zones. The project designed to test capitalism in the socialist context proved a great success and Shenzhen has since developed into one of the fastest-growing and most-developed cities in China.

Shenzhen has many things to attract people. It has one of China's two stock exchanges, the other is in Shanghai. It is the country's second largest port after Shanghai and the world's fourth busiest port. Shenzhen is the world's largest manufacturing base and home to many domestic and foreign high-tech companies, including Lenovo, Apple, and IBM. It is an immigrant city, gathering a large number of well-educated people from all over the country and also a large number of poorly educated workers from rural areas, making it, in a sense, a city of extremes. Shenzhen is also a young city with an average age of less than 30. Most interesting of all, it is the only city in Guangdong province where Mandarin is the

The skyline of Shenzhen
(Reprinted with the permission of GettyImages)

most commonly spoken language since its residents come from all over China. Shenzhen is therefore something of a melting pot for the many diverse cultures of China, a fact that can sometimes be looked upon as meaning that it has no culture. That is Shenzhen uniqueness, rarely found elsewhere in China.

Part Three

Into the Chinese Business World

Chapter

7 *Guanxi* Talks

With China's rapid economic growth and its huge market opening up to the outside world, the Chinese term *guanxi* appears so frequently in English-language texts that it is no longer a strange word. Nevertheless, this term sounds intimidating to many non-Asian businessmen for its complicated and intricate implications. This chapter explores *guanxi* from different perspectives, including its connotations, features, functions, and how it differs from Western networks. We will also provide suggestions on how to initiate, develop, and maintain quality *guanxi*.

DIMENSIONS OF *GUANXI*

As you've read in previous chapters, Chinese culture is basically people-based and relationship-oriented, valuing loyalty, accountability, and obligation. *Guanxi* is a notion derived from the basics of this culture and plays a vital role in every aspect of people's lives, including daily business practices. Its importance can be reflected in its word formation: *guan* and *xi*. The former by itself means a gate or a juncture of strategic importance, while the latter stands for a link or ties. Put together, the word literally means to "pass the gate and get connected" (Lee and Dawes 2005). In English, the word is roughly translated as "connection," "relationship," "network," or "insiders' circle," although none of these words can exactly convey its intricate and subtle implications.

Guanxi in the Past and Present

The importance of *guanxi* to the Chinese can be traced back to the traditional concept of family and group cohesiveness in Confucian philosophy. For the Chinese, individuals are part of the collective family whole, which is the source of identity, protection, trust, and strength. Such functions are realized through the contributions of all the family's individual members. In ancient times, when hardships, wars, or social chaos struck, family cohesiveness was a bastion against the brutal outside world in which no one could be trusted and relied upon. As time went by, family ties developed and expanded to other households and larger communities through marriage or other means. Such expanded *guanxi* could effectively help its members deal with hardships and difficult times. Fortunately, if a member became a government official, other members would gain from the privileges the position entailed and even prosper. An old Chinese saying aptly mirrors this *guanxi* functionality: "*Yi ren de dao, ji quan sheng tian.*" The basic meaning is, "If one prospers, those related will prosper as well." Remember in Chapter 5 how Huizhou merchants invested in education and sent more of their juniors to take the imperial civil service exams? They were actually investing in future *guanxi* networks.

Even though the social and economic situation in China now is different from the past, the tradition of personal connections remains strong. One reason is that China is still in the process of building and improving its legal framework in the context of globalization. In this period of transition, political and administrative interference remains widespread. People sometimes have to use *guanxi* "as a social means to overcome political, economic, and legislative obstacles" (Lee and Anderson 2007).

Guanxi Multiples

Basically, *guanxi* in Chinese refers to multiple links connecting individuals that have something in common. As a social being, an individual

Multi-layered *Guanxi*

Chinese is generally a member of several *guanxi* networks that may be cohesive or loose, strong or weak, deep or shallow, social-affective or instrumental. Family is the most powerful or strongest *guanxi* while the lesser ones can be a group of people who attend the same school or university, work for the same organization, serve in the same military unit, belong to the same association, or even come from the same city or province. Hence, one's personal friends, friends of friends, former classmates, relatives, or associates with shared interests can all be the members of one's various *guanxi* networks.

Guanxi is not static. At different life stages, one may walk away from or lose some old *guanxi* and join new ones. In this way, two strangers can establish *guanxi* if they have similar interests or shared aims. Since like meets like, some *guanxi* networks have more power or influence than others in social functions. A successful person, especially in the fields of politics and business, must be affiliated with some networks that are composed of other similarly successful people. In this sense, the quality and extent of one's *guanxi* networks can be used to define an individual's place in the social structure.

FYI

Guanxi is an important asset for an individual Chinese. Having more *guanxi* or not is a way to judge a person's degree of success, as wealth and other forms of social recognition would be. Some people may like to brag about their *guanxi* networks, boasting the actual truth. Their bragging may earn others' respect, give them *mianzi*/face, and bring some short-term political or monetary gains. As a foreigner trying to enter the market through *guanxi*, you need to be aware of these types of risks. Our advice is to be careful and use your best judgment. Read our suggestions on how to establish *guanxi* in China to your business advantage.

Guanxi is reciprocal and exclusive. To the people belonging to the same *guanxi* networks, all members are insiders who should not only obtain and enjoy favor and privilege but should also lend assistance whenever and wherever necessary or possible. In other words, one must contribute in order to benefit. To other networks, they are outsiders and are unlikely to obtain favors from insiders. Likewise, they have no obligations to offer a hand in times of need.

Within *guanxi*, members may not be the same in terms of contributing power. Some have higher social positions and more social resources, enabling them to do more than others. Like a family where the elder brother has to take care of the younger ones, the stronger members have obligations to help the weaker ones, although the weaker ones should not take others' help for granted. This is especially true with those deep, long-standing, and social-affective *guanxi* networks.

Chinese *Guanxi* and Western Network

It is true that networking is an important notion to Westerners as well. They have churches, alumni associations, and clubs of various kinds that connect people together. But compared to Chinese *guanxi*, Western networks are weak and loose. For example, few in such a network are willing to do a favor for others at the expense of their own interests or sacrifice the benefits of their own companies. Few will think of paying back the favor they have received. Almost nobody will take risks and do something illegal to extend favors to other members in the network. But all these can happen in China.

Compared with Western networks, each Chinese *guanxi,* especially instrumental ones, has its own unique code of ethics, tactics, and etiquette (Yang 1994). The most important one is mutual obligation and dependency. In this sense, *guanxi* is a relationship that involves constant, reciprocal exchanges of assistance and favors among its members. When one person does a favor for another within the *guanxi*, that person usually expects to receive a favor or something of similar value, if not larger, in return at some future date. For example, a gift-giver may expect a favor in return from the recipient who may have power or influence and can bring him political, social, monetary, or career advantages. By the same token, the receiving party should feel obligated to give or return the favor. Sometimes the favor may be returned at the expense of the giver's own interest and to his own disadvantage. Favor-giving here is usually treated by the Chinese as some kind of social investment upon which the giver may later draw in the *guanxi* system. If one does not follow this give-and-receive rule, that person will eventually be kicked out of the network. This is exactly what is meant by an old Chinese saying "*Lai er wu wang fei li ye* (Only receiving without giving is not decorous)." Primarily because of this, some Chinese are afraid of receiving help or favors from others because they don't want to be in too deep a social debt that they may not be able to pay back.

To you, a non-Chinese, such a give-and-receive game is especially hard to play since you have little idea about the value of the favor you have received and in what way and to what extent you should reciprocate.

The reciprocal nature of *Guanxi*

For example, when you have received a gift or favor from a Chinese, he or she views it as something unusually valuable, but you may consider it just a token of friendship or simply wonder why that particular person has given it to you. If you happily accept it, you will be expected to repay it in one way or another. However, you would probably not be fully aware of the extent of this obligation and even less aware of when and how he expects that obligation to be discharged.

CASE STUDY

Receiving and returning favors

An American Fulbright Professor was teaching American Literature at the English Department of a Chinese university. On Christmas Eve, he received an expensive Christmas gift from the department head. He was deeply moved and felt honored for being thought of by the department chair during the holiday season when he was alone and far away from home. When school started in the spring, the department chair approached him and asked if he could provide an Affidavit of Support to sponsor his son to go to a graduate school in America. This was certainly too big a favor to ask and few Americans can take such legal and financial responsibility for a person they have never met before. It suddenly dawned on the American Professor why the chair had given him that expensive Christmas gift. Of course, he did not sign the document and kept puzzling over why his Chinese colleague could have expected him to shoulder this heavy obligation. The department chair on the other hand did not understand why this American refused to help him after accepting the expensive gift.

In this case, there are at least two factors that account for this unhappy ending. One is that the Chinese and the American viewed a legal document like the Affidavit of Support differently. For the Chinese, it was just a piece of paper and the American professor would only provide the sponsorship in name. But the American believed that he would be responsible for the young man's financial situation after signing the document. The second factor is the discrepancy in understanding about the give-and-receive rules in a *guanxi* network. After the American professor happily accepted the gift from his Chinese colleague, the latter assumed that the former was willing to build up a closer *guanxi* with him and should of course return his favor by signing the document, which in his eyes, was not a big deal at all. Unfortunately, the American professor did not think that way.

GUANXI AND BUSINESS OPERATIONS IN CHINA

In Chinese business circles, *guanxi* is the network of relationships established and maintained among business partners, such as suppliers, distributors, buyers, sellers, clients, banks, and local governments. These ties link them together for mutual support and benefit. The Chinese prefer to work with people they know and trust, whereas Western businessmen choose their partners primarily based on business deals. It's true that people in the West also work with people they know and trust, but they don't count on it so much as the Chinese do. In the West it is possible to do business with a stranger if both sides can be convinced that cooperation or collaboration can bring mutual benefits. In China, however, it is almost impossible.

To some of you *guanxi* may sound like a synonym for corruption, back-door and under-the-counter deals. According to a survey conducted by Lee and Anderson (2007), *guanxi* in China can help a business get to know the key people and approach them directly, buy cheaper products, save time and energy, receive important information, know the bottom line of their competitor's bids, obtain orders, or take customers from competitors. This survey reveals that *guanxi* can be the cause of corruption and bribery. But their research also indicates that in most cases *guanxi* only functions as an entrance and business capability remains essential to overall success. We strongly discourage you from dealing in a power-money-favor game, which is in contravention of the laws of China as well as your own country. What we encourage you to do is to build healthy *guanxi* networks.

To build a possible *guanxi*, you need to bear the following in mind:

- *Guanxi* is legal in China. It is not necessarily associated with bribery or other corruption practices, so you don't have to feel uncomfortable about it.
- *Guanxi* networks are not official organizations and most of them are invisible to outsiders.
- *Guanxi* can be quite exclusive. It is a line separating insiders from outsiders. Such a division constitutes an obstacle for newcomers like you from a foreign country.
- *Guanxi* is penetrable. Since it is intertwining in nature, it is fluid and unfixed. A person belonging to different *guanxi* can work as a go-between and bring together two parties originally from two different *guanxi* networks.
- *Guanxi* is based on personal rather than institutional connections.

Based on these points, our conclusion is that building healthy and quality *guanxi* is not easy but not impossible.

According to Chen and Chen (2004), there are three stages involved in building a quality *guanxi* network: initiating, building, and using. In the initiating stage, a *guanxi* seeker should try to find common ties with the *guanxi* target by disclosing his personal background at personal or social gatherings. The personal background can include the hometown where one was born and grew up, schools attended, companies worked for, and so on. Such self-disclosure can trigger the other party to recall past experiences and help both sides identify some mutual bases, someone known to both, a similar aspiration in business or life, or common interest or hobby. However, if the other party does not respond to such a disclosure, one possibility is that he is not interested in developing a *guanxi* network.

In the *guanxi* building stage, the primary goal is to enhance the quality of the established *guanxi* and try to advance into the inner circle. According to Chen and Chen (2004), two types of activities can be performed to achieve this purpose: expressive and instrumental. The former refers to attending more social-oriented activities, such as parties, clubs gatherings, and golf, so that you have more opportunities to be close to the *guanxi* target and let both sides know each other better. The latter refers to helping each other in terms of business information exchanges, work cooperation, and so on. Through these two types of activities, both parties can build up more trust, friendliness, and obligations with a long-term orientation.

In the third stage of maintaining the *guanxi*, one can harvest one's investment, repay equity, and at the same time re-evaluate the quality of the *guanxi* network. Nevertheless, be careful when you decide to use your *guanxi*. First of all, you need to assess whether problems can be resolved through normal channels or by yourself. If your answer is no, you then estimate all your *guanxi* networks and judge which is the most suitable one for your needs. Don't exhaust all your *guanxi* since you may have other problems ahead. When you are asked to give help to your *guanxi*

Table 7.1 A model of the *guanxi*-building process

Guanxi stages	Objectives	Activities	Operation
Initiating	Setting up bases	Familiarizing	Mutual self-disclosure
Building	Enhancing quality	Expressive & instrumental transactions	Dynamic reciprocity
Using	Getting benefits and Re-evaluating *guanxi* quality	Exchanging favors	Long-term quality

Source: Chen and Chen. "On the Intricacies of the Chinese *Guanxi*: A Process Model of *Guanxi* Development," *Asia Pacific Journal of Management* 21 (2004): 305–324.

members, you are being tested to see if you are a good member of the
guanxi network. So don't be too calculating, always bear in mind *guanxi* is
a natural long-term process.

There are other ways to build and strengthen *guanxi* networks.

- Try to find a go-between to cross the dividing line and become an
  insider. Many multinational companies hire Chinese employees
  who know the language and culture, and above all are one of the
  insiders of a more powerful and influential network. Multinational
  companies also have their own methods. McKinsey has plenty of
  former employees who have moved into senior posts at other companies, becoming a valuable network for company development in
  China (Balfour 2007).
- As a token of appreciation for what your Chinese partner has done
  for you, you can offer your help by giving suggestions and sharing
  experience with the Chinese company for its overseas development.
  Or you can convince the government that what you are doing in
  China is beneficial to local economic development.
- Since *guanxi* is built upon long-standing trust, express your long-
  term interest in doing business with your partners. It is vital to
  developing and maintaining *guanxi* networks.
- You should keep frequent contact with your past business partners
  and Chinese friends to foster long-term understanding and emotional bonds, since the Chinese often feel obligated to do business
  with their friends first.
- Since *guanxi* is based on a personal network, if the person you
  know well and with whom you have cultivated a good relationship suddenly leaves your partner company, your business will
  be negatively affected and you will have to establish a new *guanxi*
  with a new person. Likewise, the person you send to do business in
  China should stay there for some time. If you change personnel, the
  guanxi established may fall apart with the person departing. In an
  interview, the president of Carrefour China mentioned an incident
  in Taiwan when he had just taken over the office there. The Taiwan-
  ese company wanted to break the old contract with Carrefour
  Taiwan simply because the person who signed the contract had left
  (Child 2006).

The following case is more illustrative of the importance of *guanxi*
establishment.

CASE STUDY

King of *Guanxi*

Mr. Vincent Lo is the Chairman of the Shui On Group, a building materials and construction firm with headquarters in Hong Kong. He is considered one of the most successful foreign investors in China by *The Economist* and CNN International Business. He is crowned as the King of *Guanxi* by the media. In an interview with a CNN reporter, Lo said: "Connections and relationships are important everywhere and they are especially important in China, because the rule of law there is not as strong as in the West. People have to rely on personal relationships a lot."

Lo started investing in China in 1985 when few people outside China dared to do so. The first project he undertook was to build a hotel in partnership with the Shanghai Communist Youth League. When the latter could not make the investment, he helped out. His act won him the long-term trust of the Chinese government. According to a report in *The Economist* (September 24, 2004), what has made Lo connect so well with the government is his "avowed desire ... to contribute to China's success and not just his own." He travels to China often to show his commitment there. He often plays golf with his Chinese partners to consolidate the *guanxi* and promote his business ideas.

With the trust and long-term commitment to China's economic development, he won the rights to develop part of the old downtown area in Shanghai. Now known as Xintiandi, the area is a 20,000-square-meter complex of restaurants, bars, and shops and is a prime entertainment spot in the city. Lo is now expanding his business to inland China and has achieved great success. Lo is an example of someone who can go from an outsider of Mainland China to an insider. He has been an honorary citizen of Shanghai since 1999 and a member of one of the top advisory committees for the central government.

SUMMARY

According to a survey of Chinese businessmen conducted by Lee and Anderson in 2007, most of the participants believe that *guanxi* is an essential element for business operations in China. The survey results also revealed that only a small percentage liked the *guanxi* game and enjoyed using it. So you are not alone if you don't like *guanxi*. You may wonder why *guanxi* should still exist and play such an important role if few people like it. You may also wonder whether *guanxi* will become less important as China's economic climate improves with a legal framework established according to international norms. We understand your question but cannot give a definite answer. Looking at Hong Kong, Taiwan, and Chinese communities overseas, *guanxi* still plays an important role. In other words, *guanxi* as a tradition will not go away, although it will operate to a lesser degree in the context of globalization that will significantly undermine political and administrative interference in China.

Chapter

8

Give Face to Others to Earn Success for Yourself

A ccording to research by Buckley et al. (2006), *guanxi* and *mianzi* ("face") are the two most prominent cultural characteristics for business operations in China. In the previous chapter exploring the notion of *guanxi*, you gained an understanding of Chinese business culture and practice. In this chapter we focus on its associated notion: *mianzi*, which means "face." First, we elaborate on the meaning of the term in relation to everyday life and business practice. We then offer suggestions for coping with possible obstacles that may arise from the issue of face. Two case studies further illustrate the importance of face to business success.

WHAT IS FACE?

Everyone has a physical face that tells others if one is attractive, plain, or somewhere in between. Everyone has a social face as well. This social face is known as *mianzi* in Chinese, which in English we refer to as "face." Face is defined as "an image of self delineated in terms of approved social attributes" (Goffman 1955) or "one's dignity, self-respect, and prestige"

A man with many faces

(Hofstede and Bond 1988). It exists and is displayed in relation to other people. It can be shown directly and indirectly, consciously and unconsciously, through one's dialect, accent, conversation topics, brands of clothes, attitudes towards friends, relationship with parents, social networks, and so on. All these are indicators of one's family background, educational level, employment, income, living standards, social status, and connections, which in turn help others form a general opinion about a person as a social being.

To most people, social face is more important than physical face, since the latter is given by genetics and there's not much one can do about it, except perhaps through plastic surgery. Social face, however, represents one's social recognition and reputation, which can be enhanced through one's own efforts. Face is a universal phenomenon but it seems more important to the Chinese as they are living in a highly hierarchical culture where an individual is more concerned with how others look at him and if they are willing to build a social network or *guanxi* in his favor. Furthermore, Chinese society emphasizes group value. An individual's face is closely related to the honor of one's groups, including family, work place, and school. In interactions with foreigners, face is associated with national pride and thus becomes even more sensitive. In a word, the Chinese consider it important to have face and maintain face anywhere and anytime.

FYI

Many Chinese sayings related to face can reveal how important it is:

♦ *"Ren huo yi zhang lian, shu huo yi zhang pi"* (A person needs face as a tree needs bark). Meaning, if one has no face, it is like a tree with no bark and will die soon after.

♦ *"Da zhong lian chong pangzi"* (One slaps one's own face until it's swollen in an effort to appear more imposing)

♦ *"Si yao mianzi huo shouzui"* (One would rather suffer and die than lose face).

How Face Functions

Face among the Chinese can function as a prized commodity or soft power. It can be given, earned, saved, exchanged, lost, or taken away. For example, face can be given by praising someone for his good work in front of peers, colleagues, or superiors, by thanking someone for doing a good job or for giving a helping hand, by showing due respect to an elder, a superior, or business partner, by presenting an appropriate gift, or by making a desirable concession. Face can also be given by helping someone avoid an embarrassing situation, for example, taking responsibility for a superior's wrong decision. Face can also be exchanged. The above face-giving actions can function as a form of social equity and will be rewarded with future face-giving acts from others. This is also why the expression "giving face" (*gei mianzi*) can often be heard among the Chinese within their social interactions.

Nevertheless, on some occasions, face is given for a purpose that cannot be publicly announced but can be subtly felt and understood by people involved. For example, in playing a board game, person A may allow his opponent, person B, to win even though person A is clearly a much better player. Why is A doing this? It may be because B is his father, whom person A wants to please, his boss, to whom A needs to show respect, or his business partner, with whom A wants to develop a business relationship. By losing the game, A believes that B's face is saved in public, and B will repay this social debt to A sometime in the future. Reading this scenario, you may think that the Chinese are not frank or honest. Nevertheless, the act of face giving and saving is a way to preserve a smooth and harmonious relationship. A game is only a game if it does not do harm to others. Here we would like to remind you of the basic principle of *The Art of War* by Sun Zi, as discussed in Chapter 4: "To win without fighting is best." Don't you think it is a perfect application here?

Face is also like a fragile commodity that can be lost by oneself or caused to be lost by other people. For example, a person can lose face by not living up to others' expectations, by failing to keep a promise, by giving the wrong answer in public, or by behaving disreputably. One can cause others to lose face by insulting or criticizing them harshly in public, refusing to offer help when requested, saying no frankly or directly, refusing another's kindness or sincere invitations, showing temper in public, behaving aggressively and arrogantly, and not treating others according to their status.

Being willing to give others face is considered a virtue among the Chinese, especially to those senior in age or rank. It is one of the major criteria for judging people. Those who don't like to give face are considered rude and uncaring; consequently few people want to develop further social relations with them. But a question may arise here: How do you balance giving face and maintaining integrity as an honest person? There is no easy formula for every situation. It depends on your own analysis, common sense, and judgment. As a foreigner doing business with the Chinese, you should perform face-giving acts whenever the situation warrants. This is an essential way to develop and foster long-term *guanxi* and extend it from an instrumental one to an affective one in wider social and business networks.

Face-giving acts may also cause confusion, for example, sometimes you can't tell if your Chinese partner's answer to your direct request or question means yes or no. On other occasions, you may find that your Chinese partner does not do what he has promised, for example, mailing a product sample to you or arranging a meeting with an important person. Such lack of action may cause inconvenience to you and your business, but it is possible that your Chinese partners are reluctant to accept your terms. In order not to make you feel a loss of face, he will avoid saying an outright "No," expecting that you will be able to figure out for yourself that he is in fact saying "No." Likewise, in the second scenario, the Chinese side may feel uncomfortable directly rejecting your request. By avoiding a straightforward "No," the Chinese side believes that the face of both parties has been saved, at least so on the surface level. The two cases provided at the end of the chapter will give you further illustration.

The subtlety of face in daily and business communication aside, one's attitude towards one's own face can also be used as a criterion to assess an

Does this stolid face mean yes or no?

individual's credibility. According to Hu (1994), those Chinese who value their own face are more reliable and can be better trusted as a means to gain access to more social networks—face is "worth more than a fortune." In this sense, face is like a living name card. Traditionally, fear of losing face formed the basis for the informal system of contracts and agreements between businesses and customers (Redding and Ng 1982). In Chapter 5 on the roots of Chinese business culture, we mentioned Qiao Zhiyong, a Shanxi merchant who successfully collected money from his neighbors for his tea-trading trip. This was not bound by a legal document but based on his credibility or the face he had established and valued for a long time as a person and businessman. A similar story relates how a well-known Huizhou merchant sold all his property to repay his debt to those who had lent money to him before his death. To him, his face or reputation was more important than anything. He would not let others take away his good name even after his death. In the eyes of many Chinese one's face and a company's reputation provide a far better guarantee than a legal document. This is also why the Chinese like to do business with people they trust. The next chapter will discuss this in greater detail.

HOW TO DEAL WITH FACE-RELATED ISSUES

The Chinese care so much about face because it is closely related to Confucianism. Accepting and respecting a person's face or social position through correct conduct is one way to keep society functional and well ordered. Refusing to do so may pose a challenge to a person's position in the hierarchy, especially so if the person is your superior, senior, or business partner. Giving face is a way of protecting one's social self in order to function as an integral part of the social network. Causing someone to lose face is not merely a matter of personal embarrassment; it may even disrupt the social order and damage the integrity of the group's value. This is why the Chinese are very careful with face-related situations, even though it may sometimes be against their own wishes or at the expense of their own personal integrity. See the two case studies below on Westerners' experiences of working in China.

CASE STUDY

Experiences with face when working in China

Peter is a department manager working in the Chinese branch of a large Western company in Beijing. He frequently found an error message popping up when he saved a file on his computer. His Chinese colleague would help with the problem. One day he happened to find that he should have saved the file in another way and shared his finding with his Chinese colleagues. To his surprise, everybody knew the solution. He was very curious and asked them why they had not told him earlier. To his surprise, they told him that they were his subordinates and that pointing out the mistake would directly damage his face as the boss.

Bill is an American working as a technician in a joint-venture company in China. He found that every project report always had the same sentence: "Under the leadership of the company management team, our group has achieved ..." He asked his Chinese colleague why they always included this sentence since nobody from the management level had taken part in the project. He got the answer that people should give face to their superiors and boss. Soon afterwards, a small accident happened due to inappropriate machine operation. Thus Bill wrote in the accident report: "Under the leadership of our company's management team, the accident happened ..." His Chinese colleague patiently explained to him when this sentence should be used and when it should not be used, finally helping Bill understand the intricate meaning of the notion face.

A common error committed by foreign business people is to fail to treat people properly according to rank and title. To avoid this, you need to know exactly who is who before starting your initial business talks. Failure to do so can make both sides lose face. Another common error is that Westerners may offend a Chinese unintentionally by making fun of them in a way that may be acceptable in someone's country but is inappropriate to the Chinese. So be careful when cracking jokes with your Chinese business counterpart or friends. Another thing you need to keep in mind is that in business interactions a person's face is not simply his own but that of the entire organization he represents. Your relationship with an individual and the respect you accord will probably be crucial to your business success in China. One more thing that you need to pay attention to in this respect is to avoid openly criticizing China's political and legal systems, complaining about any inconveniences you have come across while staying in China, or mentioning any inefficiencies on the part of your Chinese partners. Although your Chinese friends or partners may hold the same opinion, they may not want to hear such criticism from foreigners. This will cause them to lose face and hurt their national pride.

HOW TO SAY "NO" TACTFULLY

Some people say the American style of communication can be compared to an arrow: direct, candid, straightforward, and to the point. In most cases, "yes" means yes and "no" means no. Unlike Americans, the Chinese grow up with a Confucian way of thinking: Do not say no directly to anyone, otherwise you will offend people and damage their face. As discussed above, face, which represents self-dignity, is a major concern for the Chinese when communicating with people. By giving a direct "No" you will make the other party lose face, which may result in direct confrontation and eventually the loss of business.

FYI

There are times that you need to say "No": when somebody praises your work; when you are offered a gift; when you are invited to a party. In these situations, despite being happy and eager to accept, try to be restrained, otherwise you will be considered greedy and lose face.

Instead of saying "no" directly, you can reply with expressions like "maybe" and "I'll have to think about that." This communication style is called *wan zhuan* (euphemism) in Chinese. It is a non-confrontational, non-provoking, non-threatening but graceful and polite way of not saying "yes." So if you hear phrases, such as "No big problems," this would usually indicate that problems do exist. As a foreigner, first, you should do as the Chinese do and avoid saying "no" directly since there are many other ways to express disagreement. Secondly, you should learn to read between the lines and detect the hidden "no" conveyed to you from your Chinese counterpart. Here are some typical sentences indicating "no":

- We need more time to think about your request or give more thought later.
- We cannot make a decision before consulting with superiors. We will have to check with them first.
- That might be difficult.
- It could be a problem.
- I can foresee problems here.
- I am not sure about that one.
- This is the first request of this kind we have had.
- It is certainly worth thinking about.
- We will think it over.
- Let us discuss this another time.
- Leave it with me and we will consider it.
- It may not be a convenient time.
- There is no responsible person around.
- The matter is under consideration.

Please be alert to these types of remarks. You can ask politely in further discussion if the answer is negative. In many cases, the Chinese side may give you a more detailed explanation. The explanation may help you identify where the problem is, to whom you can turn, and what should be done to fix the problem.

CASE STUDY

The case of the missing labels

An Oregon company placed a purchase order with a Chinese import and export company in Fujian. When the shipment arrived, the US Customs Service did not allow the cargo to enter the United States because there were no labels attached to the items showing the country of origin. The Oregon company had to label the goods itself so that the shipment could be released from Customs. This Oregon company was unhappy about the situation because the labels had been specified in the company's letter of credit, which is the equivalent of a contract. Since there would be more Chinese shipments coming later, the Oregon company faxed a letter to the Fujian company: "We have received the shipment that we ordered. According to the L/C, it was your responsibility to label each item but you failed to do so. To correct your mistakes, we had to spend extra money and time re-labeling the goods. Please be sure to put labels on each item in your next shipment."

Weeks passed and there was no response. Later, when the second shipment came, the same thing happened. The Oregon company had no way out but to seek advice from experts. The company then wrote another letter to Fujian: "We have just received the second shipment from you. We are happy that our order has arrived on time. The quality of your product is excellent. Thank you very much for your efforts to make all this happen. I hope we can have further cooperation in the future. By the way, there is a small problem I wish you could help solve ..." The Oregon company in this letter also informed the Chinese side about extra time and money they spent on correcting the labeling error and expressed the hope that the Chinese side would consider some compensation. Two days later, the Oregon company received a fax from Fujian. In the fax the Chinese side expressed their regret for what had happened and promised to give a 30% discount on the company's next order to make up for the loss. One month later, another shipment came with all the labels on. The Chinese company did what had been promised.

What was wrong with the first letter? The Oregon company did not give face to the Fujian company by expressing its dissatisfaction about the labeling problem in an improper tone. This letter made the Chinese side feel that they had committed a terrible mistake— a huge loss of face. If the Oregon company had been aware of the face factor and used more polite and circuitous language, the Chinese side would not have felt embarrassed or lost face; they would have been more than willing to help solve the problem. Remember, making your Chinese partner feel a loss of face will not help solve a problem. Fortunately, this Oregon company changed its strategy and reversed the situation.

CASE STUDY

The case of the missing "No"

An American business woman was negotiating with her Chinese counterpart over an import agreement. However, one of her terms was unacceptable to the Chinese side. When the American woman mentioned this again during another round of negotiation, the Chinese representative said that her request would need further consideration by the Chinese side. The businesswoman offered to further clarify the matter and asked for detailed reasons why the Chinese side disagreed. The Chinese representative mentioned certain problems and difficulties, but still gave her the response "*kaolü kaolü*" which means "We'll think this over again" or "We must give it more thought." You can imagine what happened a few days later: the Chinese side still refused to accept her terms.

Why didn't the Chinese representative just say "no" in the first place? Because stating his position directly would mean denying her request, which in turn would damage his face as he was committed to the moral principle of staying in harmony with others. It would also damage her face by contradicting her status as a business partner. The American woman felt frustrated at the final word from the Chinese side. She thought if only he had said no earlier and had explained why it was impossible she would have tried to figure out some other way to make a better deal. Her Chinese counterpart, however, was concerned about his face and her face. He believed that avoiding loss of face was more important than making a deal in that round of negotiation and therefore never said "No" directly.

SUMMARY

Based on the above discussion, you can see that face can play both a positive role (keeping a harmonious relationship) and a negative role (causing communication confusion). However, in China, face is a necessary condition for the smooth running of business interactions. This is further corroborated by an on-line survey conducted by the Sina Corporation (1998). Out of 1,235 responses, 83.2% considered that face is very important in social interactions and only 2.7% thought it is not important. Although 27.8% agreed that "it is cultural rubbish and should be done away with," 15.7% thought "it is very good; good for communication with others," and 52% suggested that "it is neither good nor bad; it is useful anyway."

As a conclusion to this chapter, we would like to cite the eight guidelines laid out in *Encountering the Chinese* by Hu Wenzhong and Cornelius Grove (Hu and Grove 1998, 121–22) to recapitulate the rules we have discussed in this chapter:

1. Be deferential to those above you by virtue of age or position.
2. Be considerate of those below you by virtue of age or position.
3. Do not expect that a Chinese will act contrary to group norms.
4. Do not insist that your host respect your rights or opinions.
5. Do not in any way defy your host's accepted moral standards.
6. Do not show anger; avoid confrontations.
7. If you must say no, try to do so as tactfully as possible.
8. If you must criticize, do so in private and with expressions of positive regard.

Chapter

9 In the Eyes of Each Other

W e all have certain stereotypical images of people from different countries or ethnic groups, formed under the influence of movies, books, our own experiences, and the experiences of others. While our aim in this book is to help you establish an image of the Chinese, at least in general terms, it is also useful for you to know how the Chinese perceive foreigners. This chapter investigates various aspects of how foreigners are received in China, as well as summarizes the general image foreigners have of the Chinese and the types of Chinese people you may encounter on your visits to China.

HOW THE CHINESE RECEIVE FOREIGNERS

From 1949, when the People's Republic of China was founded, to 1978, when China started to implement the open-door policy, China was closed to the outside world. Ordinary Chinese knew little about what was going on outside China. They didn't know, for example, that in certain parts of the world ordinary blue-collar workers drove a car to work, owned their own home, and so on. To the average Chinese a bicycle was considered valuable. During those 30 years, and even the initial years of the open-door policy, Chinese citizens were not allowed to converse with foreigners. If anyone did, he or she might be suspected of disclosing state secrets and arrested as a result.

With the implementation of the open-door policy in the late 1970s, foreigners began to come to China for business, academic exchange, and vacations. Since few Chinese could go abroad in those days, these foreigners opened a window for ordinary Chinese to see the outside world. They brought in advanced technologies, Western ideologies, and modern ways of life, which opened the eyes of the Chinese, especially intellectuals and young people, to new and exciting possibilities. Foreigners in the street would often be surrounded by a crowd of curious onlookers wanting to see how they dressed, talked, and so on. Nowadays such scenes rarely occur in big cities, thanks to 30 years of opening-up to the outside world. The Chinese have become accustomed to foreigners living, working, and traveling alongside them. Some of them have even made foreign friends. Foreigners are still foreigners, however, which means in general terms they are received rather differently from the way one Chinese receives another Chinese.

Honorable Guests and Special Treatment

China is traditionally a nation upholding hospitality and ceremonies. From a young age, Chinese children are told to be generous and hospitable to visitors and guests in order not to lose face in front of outsiders. This is particularly so with foreign visitors. There are a number of old sayings in the Chinese language on how to receive friends and guests. One of the most oft-quoted at official welcome parties for foreign guests is from *Analects of Confucius*: "*You peng zi yuan fang lai, bu yi le hu* (We are extremely happy when there are friends coming from afar)."

The Chinese tend to give foreign guests and business partners the best treatment they can. Before you arrive, your Chinese host will make a detailed plan for your stay. While you are in China you will be shown around local beauty spots, invited to lavish banquets, and taken to performances of Chinese operas or acrobatics. If you get lost in the street, there are always warm-hearted people willing to offer help. In a crowded bus or subway you may be offered a seat while a pregnant woman may stand nearby. An American business person who has been to many countries once told us that China is the most hospitable country in the world.

Even so, you still need to be aware of some important aspects of China and the Chinese. First of all, you need to learn something about China, including its history, culture, people, and then find opportunities to show off your knowledge to your Chinese host. This book can be one of your resources. Your knowledge, understanding, and appreciation of Chinese culture will be a great boon to your business success in China. Secondly, as more and more foreigners come to China they no longer attract much attention in big cities, although in small cities and remote areas they may still be surrounded and stared at by curious people. You may be called as "long nose" (*da bizi*), "foreign devil" (*yang guizi*), or "foreigner" (*lao wai*). Remember, there is no negative connotation in these "titles." If you find yourself the center of curiosity, however uncomfortable it may make you feel, please learn to get used to it and live with it. People are simply interested in you because of your difference from the people they see every day. Thirdly, please remember while in China that you are welcomed and treated as a guest. The implication here is that you are an outsider. If you want to be an insider of important *guanxi* circles, you will need to spend more time and make more effort to learn the rules. As we pointed out in the chapters on *guanxi* and face, reciprocity is the key word here.

Friend, Family Member, or Business Partner

While you are in China, don't be surprised if you are referred to as "long-standing friend" by your Chinese partner, even though you have only known each other for a couple of days. Remember the sentence often quoted at welcome ceremonies: "We are extremely happy when there are friends coming from afar." The Chinese tend to generalize the words "friends" and "friendship," not only in reference to foreigners, but to other Chinese as well. It is a quick way to show goodwill and build a relationship. In the same way, they tend to show care and concern, as a friend would, and as your friend also ask you for a hand and suggestions in return, as illustrated in the following case study.

CASE STUDY

Is business only business?

An American company wanted to acquire a Chinese company to speed up its market penetration in China. After several rounds of pre-negotiation contacts, the American company sent a team to China to negotiate the details of the deal. After both sides sat down at the table for the first time, they started with some small talk about the weather, the trip from America to China, and local food. Then the Chinese head asked the American head: "I heard that you are from Columbus, Ohio. Actually my son will go to graduate school at Ohio State University next fall." Upon hearing this, the American responded: "It's really a good school. Congratulations." Then after a few seconds he continued, "It's time for us to talk about business. Shall we start now?" The atmosphere in the room immediately froze and the talks that day did not progress as smoothly as expected.

We believe you can figure out what went wrong with the American side. If you come across a similar scenario, we believe you can do much better after reading this book. In such a situation, you can say a little bit about Columbus and the Ohio State University. You may also want to show that you care about the young man's school life in America and share your own experiences of your student days. If you think it will take up too much time during the meeting, you can suggest talking about it during the break. This is the expected way to treat a friend. Only thus will the Chinese side consider you as a friend or friend in the making. So you should act accordingly. Otherwise, what's the point of you sitting in the same room with these particular Chinese people and working towards the same goal?

Sometimes, you are regarded not only as a friend but also as a family member, just as the Chinese consider each other within the work place. The following is an interesting case to illustrate the point.

CASE STUDY

How come an American has a Chinese sister-in-law?

During a break in negotiations between a Chinese company and an American company, the team leaders from both sides had a casual chat. The Chinese head said, "Your sister-in-law is very happy that you have come to our country and wants to invite you to our home for a humble dinner." The American was totally at a loss about the word "sister-in-law," not to mention the words "humble dinner." He thought to himself that it was impossible that the Chinese head knew his sister-in-law. But to whom was he referring? After the Chinese head explained the arrangement by mentioning "your sister-in-law" several times, the American realized that this "sister-in-law" was actually the wife of the Chinese head.

Please don't laugh when you read this story. In the chapter on Confucianism we discussed the importance of family in Chinese culture. We have also mentioned that social communities are considered an extension of the family. People can refer to each other using family forms of address, such as Brother Li or Sister Zhang in the work place. On the street, people use familial titles to address each other even among strangers. It is a way to narrow the gap and show humility and respect. The Chinese head in the above story generalized the family form of address to his American partner in order to build a close family-like *guanxi* network. Since the Chinese head considered the American as his brother, his wife naturally became the American's sister-in-law.

DIFFERENT COUNTRIES, DIFFERENT IMAGES

As mentioned in Chapter 1, Western powers invaded China with guns and opium in the 19th century and destroyed the Sino-centric mentality of the Chinese. Since then, the Chinese have held a mixed attitude of pride, awe, fear, and curiosity towards people from other countries. Now, about 30 years after the launch of the open-door policy and economic reforms, the Chinese have become used to working with foreigners in business and other arenas.

Just as you will have some stereotypical images of people from different ethnic backgrounds, so Chinese people have preconceived ideas of people from other countries. For example, Americans are open, big-hearted, warm, friendly, trusting, and wealthy. American businessmen are good entrepreneurs, innovative, professional, and polite. On the other hand, they are also perceived as being somewhat superficial, impatient, pushy, and short-sighted. They like to interrupt people, don't listen enough, are too direct in asking questions, giving opinions, and poking fun, saying thanks and sorry too often, too time-conscious and deadline-driven, and do not show enough respect for formalities. Europe is viewed by the Chinese as the cultural center of Western civilization and Europeans are perceived as more refined, reserved, sophisticated, but sometimes cold and aloof compared to Americans.

As for the Japanese, the Chinese have mixed feelings. On the one hand, Japan is one of the world's economic giants. Many Chinese love the high quality of Japanese products, despite their much higher prices compared to similar products made in China. The Japanese as a people are hard-working, efficient, and extremely loyal to their firms and country, traits which many Chinese believe are the key to the country's success in economic development. On the other hand, many Chinese think that the Japanese are dominating, hegemonic, and untrustworthy. In private, quite a few Chinese don't like the Japanese because of the atrocities the Japanese army perpetrated in China during the Second Sino–Japanese War.

HOW FOREIGNERS VIEW THE CHINESE

To most people China is one of the biggest countries in the world with the largest population and a most remarkable 5,000-year-old civilization. With more and more products being made in China, the country has become a world factory churning out cheap goods for consumers around the globe. The Chinese are also viewed as a hard-working, enterprising, and clever people. You can find many Chinese working in Wall Street and Silicon Valley. The term "Chinese" also conjures up images of delicious food, Jackie Chan, Bruce Lee, gongfu, Tai Chi, fengshui, and fortune cookies.

We did a survey with some Americans on their impression of China and the Chinese. All respondents have lived in China at some point but their impressions vary greatly. Their opinions fall into two categories and the results are summarized below.

Modern China and Westernized Chinese

- China has developed so fast that every time I go there I can always find something different.
- There are a lot of opportunities there for foreigners in terms of career and business development.
- The Chinese are very international in outlook, such as fashion, Hollywood movies, and electronic devices.
- Everybody is learning English. Every time I go out, I always come across people who want to   practice English with me.
- The Chinese media cover what is happening in America every day, while CNN only occasionally mentions China.
- In Shanghai you can find everything that people consume here in the US. Sometimes I forget that I am in Shanghai, since it is so American with bars and coffee houses everywhere, not to mention KFC and MacDonald's.
- In my company, there are some young Chinese who are just like the white-collar workers here in the US, very professional and systematic.
- Every Chinese employee in my company has an English name and they prefer to be called by their English names rather than their Chinese names.
- When I speak Chinese, I always receive a surprised smile from the Chinese. I like it and feel welcomed.

Developing China and Traditional Chinese

- I stayed in Beijing for a while and went to a remote village for a research project. The difference between the two is shocking. You cannot believe they are in the same country.
- There is a serious pollution problem in urban China. It is rare to see a blue sky in winter.

- There are too many cars on Beijing streets and a lot of people drive in a reckless way.
- People eat from common dishes. I like the culture since people share.
- My Chinese friends often take me out for dinner and insist on paying for my meal.
- Some Chinese businessmen are difficult to understand, too reserved, polite, and cautious, and you never know what they are thinking.
- Chinese negotiators like to keep silent, stiff, and rigid; they often use vague words and ambiguous expressions and it is hard to know where they stand.
- Chinese negotiators are inefficient, indirect, and even dishonest at times.
- Some Chinese are ethnocentric and proud of their five thousand years of history and civilization; they think Americans are shallow because of our country's short history.
- They have too many rules of courtesy and etiquette.
- They are too quiet at social gatherings.
- They are overly attached to status, titles, and positions. There is a list of titles on the business cards and I can barely imagine how they can handle so many things at the same time.

Our Remarks on the Survey

The people who participated in our survey were widely divided in terms of their impressions and opinions about China and its people. The opinions largely depend on where, why, and how long they stayed. China is so big and interregional differences are great. The coastal cities are much more advanced and developed than the inland and rural areas. In addition, the varying opinions are to do with the people they encountered or worked with. China has undergone a social and economic transformation thanks to the open-door policy and internal economic reforms. The Chinese as a people have changed a lot but to different degrees due to various factors, such as age, education, social position, location, and income. It would be a totally different experience to work with old-fashioned Chinese than with young people who have just returned from abroad. So, if you travel to China on business you should be open-minded about what you see, hear, and experience. We will come back to this issue in the chapter on negotiation.

Chapter

10 When in China, Do as the Chinese Do

To ensure your success in China, you need to learn the basics of Chinese communication etiquette in order to understand the Chinese side of the business coin, such as getting to know people's titles, forms of address, shaking hands, and exchanging business cards. These practices may prove perplexing to those arriving in China for the first time. Nevertheless, familiarity with these hidden rules will ease the way into Chinese culture and speed up the process of adapting to the Chinese business world.

CHINESE NAMES

An English name is written and spoken with the given name coming before the family name. Chinese names reverse this order: the family name goes before the given name. Some Chinese who do business with Westerners sometimes reverse the order of their names to conform to the Western style. This can sometimes cause confusion, for example, an American receiving a business letter or email from Qiang Zhang might mistakenly begin a reply with "Dear Mr. Qiang." If you are not sure, you should try to get it straight in advance.

Another thing that may confuse you is that many Chinese have the same last names, requiring a special effort to tell who is who. There are

ZHANG: One of the most common surnames in the world

some very common family names in China, such as Wang, Zhang, Li, or Liu. It often happens that the company's CEO, marketing manager, and receptionist share the same family name without any blood connections. In this situation you have to memorize their given names in order not to confuse CEO Zhang with receptionist Zhang so that you can address each properly and respectfully.

Another confusing scenario you may encounter regarding Chinese names is that many people not only share the same family names but also the same given names. You can find thousands of people sharing the same full names such as Zhang Yang and Li Wei. If you happen to know two people with identical names, you have to memorize their personal features, such as the tall Zhang Yang or female Li Wei. The Chinese themselves use this strategy.

FORMS OF ADDRESS AND TITLES

The Chinese have titles similar to Mr., Miss, Ms., and Mrs. Please note, however, that all Chinese titles should follow either the full name or family name rather than precede it, for example Mr. Li should be Li Xiansheng. In the People's Republic of China (PRC), a married woman does not take her husband's family name. If Miss Li Hong married Mr. Zhang Qiang, she becomes Mrs. Zhang, but at the same time she remains Li Hong and prefers to be addressed so. Most people still address her as Li Hong or Ms Li. If Li Hong is not from mainland China, such as Taiwan or Hong Kong, however, she may add her husband's surname to her full name and be called Zhang Li Hong, whereas at work, she is very likely to be called Miss Li or Ms. Li.

Titles like Mr., Miss, Ms., and Madam were seldom used in the PRC after 1949 and before the early 1980s. Instead, "Comrade" was used to address all people regardless of gender or marital status. The title of comrade is seldom used now, instead titles such as Mr., Miss, Ms., and Madam have become more popular.

Official and job titles are also widely used to address people, for example, Manager, President, Chairman, General Manager, and so on. Given names are usually omitted when these titles are used. If Mr. Zhang Qiang is a manager of a company he can be addressed as Manager Zhang, not Manager Zhang Qiang. Since these titles convey the social status or designated positions of a person in society, people prefer using them in formal and sometimes informal settings rather than Mr., Miss, or Ms. in order to show respect.

Various ways of addressing Zhang Qiang

In China, people outside the family circle rarely call each other by their given names. They use formal, official, and professional titles, as explained above, or for closer acquaintances and friends they use diminutives, such as *lao*, literally meaning "old," for men only, or *xiao*, literally meaning "young," followed by the person's family name. As a foreigner, remember to use the more formal form of address, such as mister or miss, until you are sure which level is applicable. This is something that will come with time and experience.

In academic circles, government agencies, TV stations, and performing groups, *Laoshi* (literally "teacher") is often used to address people, especially older people, even if they don't actually teach. This is a respectful form of address to those who are well educated, richly experienced, and established in their field, including writers, directors, and research associates. There is another highly respectful form of address that uses the family name plus *Lao* (old), as in Li Lao or Zhang Lao, for older people who are prominent in their field.

FYI

Nowadays, young people in big cities choose to use English names, such as Jane, Jennifer, or Bob. Like Westerners, they just call each other by their English names instead of Chinese names. This practice has become especially fashionable among the younger set working in multinational companies.

CHINESE AND WESTERN HANDSHAKES

Touching, hugging, or kissing people are not customary practices among the Chinese. The Chinese way of greeting is usually just a nod or a slight bow with a light smile. Handshaking, which was imported from the West, is generally an accepted form of greeting. However, Chinese handshakes differ in two respects from those common in the West. First, the Chinese tend to shake hands very lightly, which is known as "dead fish" style, instead of gripping the hand firmly and pumping vigorously, as often seen in the West. If you encounter a handshake like this, you should immediately soften your grasp, shake, and let go or simply accept the handshake as a business formality. Second, a handshake can last as long as ten seconds, instead of the brisk three-second contact common in the West.

What we recommend is a combination of both styles, which is gaining popularity nowadays. Start with a traditional handshake and conclude with a slight bow over the two clasped and shaking hands—a perfect global bridge. Bear in mind that a soft handshake and lack of eye contact does not necessarily indicate timidity in Chinese culture.

BUSINESS CARDS — SOFT POWER AND NAME BRAND

At business meetings a handshake is always followed by a ritualistic exchange of business cards. You should always carry an ample supply of business cards, preferably with English text on one side and Chinese on the other. Seek advice from a well-educated Chinese on the choice of Chinese characters for your name and company, as some characters have better meanings than others.

The proper procedure for exchanging business cards in China is to give and receive cards with both hands, holding the card corners between thumb and forefinger with the text facing the receiver. When receiving a card, do not simply pocket it immediately, but take a few moments to study the card for what it says, even if it is only printed in Chinese. Try to say the person's name and look back with a smile at the card's owner for confirmation. The business card represents the person who gives it to you, so it should be treated with respect and dignity. Once you receive someone's business card, you should not ask for it again because by doing so you may be interpreted as not caring enough about the card, the business partner, or the business relationship. If you have misplaced the card that was given to you, the best

Business card or curriculum vitae?

face-saving way or rule of thumb is to say that you'd like to give the person's name and card to a friend or business associate of yours who may possibly use the card owner's service or business in the future.

GREETING THE CHINESE WAY

The Chinese way of saying "How do you do?" or "Hello" is simply *"Ni hao,"* which literally means "Good day" or "You are well." The question form of the same greeting is *"Ni hao ma?"* literally "Are you well?" or "How are you?" This can be used at any time of the day for greeting anyone, although it sounds a little too formal to close friends or your Chinese business associate. They normally just nod their head or smile at each other, or say *"Hai"*, which, as you may guess, is derived from English. However, Chinese people will be pleasantly surprised and appreciate it when you greet them in Chinese. They may go out of their way to help you or make it easier for you to visit, live, work, travel, or do business in the country.

Use the phrase *"Nin hao,"* as a more formal and polite form of greeting someone of high stature who is older than you and to whom you want to show respect. *Nin* is a polite form of *ni* (you), which is similar to the French *vous*, the Spanish *usted*, and the German *Sie*.

The difference between *Ni* and *Nin*

FYI

Even if you do not speak Chinese, it is always a plus to know how to say simple phrases like *"Ni hao"* to greet people. It can be used for virtually any occasion regardless of the time of day and the social status of the person you are greeting. People always respond to your *"Ni hao"* with another *"Ni hao."* In Appendix I, we provide a list of Chinese phrases and sentences that you can use when greeting your Chinese friends.

Another Chinese greeting is *"Chi le ma?"* which means "Have you eaten?" Although this greeting is in the form of a question, you do not need to answer it in an honest way just as "How are you?" used in the West is seldom answered with exact information about one's health. The way to deal with this kind of greeting is to answer either "I've eaten" or "I'm going to eat soon," depending on your situation. You can be truthful about saying you are going to eat soon because this information is not likely to elicit an invitation from the person greeting you. One exception is when you are greeted by your Chinese business partner or colleague who has extensive experience in Western culture. In this case, his or her greeting may be the beginning of an invitation to a meal and you should give a serious answer if you do not want to miss it.

Come on, that's just a greeting!

Other common greetings include *"Qu na er?"* which is literally translated as "Where are you going?" The person is not being inquisitive about your next destination or nosing into your private life because it is not actually a genuine question that requires a specific answer. This greeting is typically used when one person meets another on the street or in the neighborhood. Again, it is similar to "How are you?" in the West and is simply another way of saying *"Ni hao."* If you are greeted this way by an acquaintance, you should respond either by naming your destination or by saying vaguely, "I'm going there," while gesturing your head or hand slightly in the direction in which you are moving.

CASE STUDY

What is behind the greeting "Have you eaten"?

An American business person was on a business trip to China a few years ago. He had no idea about Chinese language or culture. Shortly after his arrival at a hotel in Beijing, he went to the bank inside the hotel to exchange some money. He was extremely surprised when the bank clerk asked him if he had had his dinner. In Western culture this question would be regarded as an indirect invitation to dinner, and between unmarried young people it indicates a young man's interest in dating a girl. From the reading above, you know this is a simple way to greet people and show goodwill. It has nothing to do with meal invitation or dating request.

Another typical form of Chinese greeting that you may find difficult to respond to is a casual statement of a fact. For example, suppose you are reading a newspaper with a cup of coffee in a café when your Chinese friend walks in. Instead of saying *"Ni hao,"* he may say something like, "Oh, you are reading newspaper" or "You are drinking coffee." Or he may ask, "Are you reading today's paper?" or "Any news in the paper?" This type of comment is just another friendly greeting.

ICE BREAKERS AND SMALL TALK

Socialization is a way of getting to know your business partner in person and establishing a *guanxi* network in China. For this reason, some topics of conversation are better than others. Safe, non-sensitive topics of conversation include the weather, size and diversity of China and your own country, places of historical interest and beauty spots, school or work, your good impression of China, Chinese customs and habits, as well as Chinese language and difficulties learning it. You can also compliment your counterpart's English proficiency, talk about Chinese arts and history, applaud China's economic reforms and the splendid progress the country has made in various aspects, such as economic development, increased living standards, and improved housing and environment. The 2008 Olympic Games in Beijing, the 2010 World Fair in Shanghai, Chinese food, Chinese medicine, daily news, sports, music, movies or entertainment events can also become good conversation topics.

Personal but safe topics are family and children. Ask if the person is married and whether or not he or she has children, if they are girls or boys, what ages, schools they attend, how well they are doing at school, college, career. You can also chat about hometowns or neighborhoods, if someone has lived in the same area all his life, or where else he has lived and worked in China. These topics are unlikely to cause any subtle cross-cultural misunderstanding and your Chinese partner will feel comfortable and talk freely with you.

As a foreigner, you are advised not to talk with Chinese about political topics, such as Tibet and Taiwan, human rights issues, power balance and struggle among current leaders and current policies, the June 4th Tiananmen crackdown, the Cultural Revolution, the *Falungong* (a forbidden sect in China), and international politics. You should avoid calling China "Communist China," "Red China," and "Mainland China." Please do not ask people about their party membership. Other conversational topics that may not be appropriate include physical appearance, such as woman's prettiness and good figure, someone's sex life. Do not ask a woman in her 20s or 30s if she is married or whether or not she has kids. Do not brag about yourself, your country, your wellbeing, and achievements. Remember that Confucianism honors humility and courtesy.

People from different cultures may have different interpretations about the word "privacy." In America, every means has been taken to protect and respect an individual's privacy, such as age, income, marital status, and so on. People try to avoid such personal topics in daily conversations. However, the Chinese have a different attitude so be prepared to answer questions tactfully. Although these questions may make you feel uncomfortable, you should never say anything that would be offensive or insulting to the Chinese, such as "It's none of your business," "Sorry, you are intruding into my privacy," "I don't want to talk about that," "I don't feel comfortable answering your question," "Why do you want to know that?" and so on.

You should know that discussing these topics is common among Chinese. Frank answers are always viewed as a sign of a close relationship.

When asked a question that you do not wish to answer, you can choose to tell the truth with some explanations. For example, if you are asked why you are divorced, you can tactfully say that it is a long story and you'll tell it another time. With such a reply, your Chinese friend can feel your hesitation. If asked about your salary, you can explain that your salary may sound high by Chinese standards but the cost of living is also high in your country. You can further elaborate by saying that your income is just about average in your country, you have to pay a mortgage loan and property tax for your house, and you have to pay income tax, which is pretty high in your country. If you are asked why you are not married at this age, you may want to tell them that you have other priorities in you life and your career is top of your list and family second.

CHINESE BODY LANGUAGE

Nonverbal communication can include facial expressions, tones of voice, gestures, and eye contact. They may convey messages missing from a verbal interaction. Relatively speaking, the Chinese are more reserved in using gestures to express emotions.

Eye Contact

When the Chinese greet someone, they do not look a person straight in the eyes. Instead, they lower their eyes slightly. This is a sign of deference and respect. Therefore, you should refrain from looking intensely into someone's eyes as this may make a Chinese person feel uncomfortable. Brief eye contact during a conversation can be made, then move your eye to either side of the other party.

Physical Contact

According to Confucian teachings, contact between men and women is prohibited, unless the two are married. People seldom hug and kiss each other, even among family members. Touching, hugging, kissing, putting your hand around the shoulder of another person, or patting someone on the back can make someone feel uncomfortable. However, lightly touching another person's arm when speaking is a sign of close familiarity. Nowadays, at least in the cities, young people are Westernized, but even so hugs and cheek kisses between men and women are seldom seen. So when you first meet your business partner, hand shaking is enough.

Silence

Silence can mean different things in different situations. Sometimes it means "No" when a person does not know how to reply to a request or does not want to say "No" to make you lose face. In conversation, long pauses are not considered improper. As a Westerner, you may feel uncomfortable with long silences, but in China you need to tolerate this.

Decoding Chinese Body Language and Gestures

Some gestures used by Chinese people may be incomprehensible to foreigners; likewise, some foreign gestures can be misunderstood by the Chinese. Below we list some of the common gestures used in Chinese culture and their meanings:

- Nodding is a common gesture among Westerners and among Chinese. But for Chinese, sometimes it does not indicate agreement, as most Westerners interpret, but a gesture of recognition with the meaning "I hear you."
- When the Chinese want someone to approach, they extend their hand palm down and curl the fingers, as if scratching an imaginary surface.
- Holding one's hand up near the face and slightly waving means "No," or it can be a mild rebuke.
- Pointing at someone with the forefinger is an accusatory motion, which is considered rude or hostile. When you point, use the entire hand with palm open.
- Winking is impolite and can have a negative connotation.
- Shaking hands is the universal form of greeting. Some Chinese make a fist with the left hand, cover it with the right palm, and shake the hands up and down when meeting with close friends or saying thanks.
- When the Chinese yawn, cough, or use a toothpick, they cover their mouths.
- In Chinese homes, people remove their shoes at the entrance. So make sure to wear clean socks when visiting a Chinese home.

Chapter

11 Behind the Negotiation Table (I)

After the initial contacts with your potential business counterpart in China, you finally arrive in the country to negotiate face to face on the specific details of the proposed deal. You will have ample opportunities throughout this process to apply what you read in this book, for example *guanxi*, face, and social hierarchy, and experience the ups and downs of the negotiation process. You may be delighted with the friendly atmosphere of a welcome banquet only to become puzzled when the sunny face of a Chinese negotiator suddenly turns stony and distant. Later you may find yourself frustrated with the seemingly never-ending negotiation process and only when departing for home with a signed contract and the goodwill of the new Chinese partner will you finally feel relieved. In this chapter we will guide you through the stages of negotiation, before, during, and after, highlighting some common issues and concerns.

WHAT IS NEGOTIATION?

Negotiation is a process of bridging the gaps between two sides, reaching agreements in terms and conditions to guide future business behavior and maximizes the mutual interests of all parties involved. According to international norms, a negotiation process is divided into three distinct phases: pre-negotiation, negotiation, and post-negotiation. Ideally, such a process should be transparent, specific, and straightforward on all points. However, this is not exactly the case with Chinese business practices.

Before China's economic reforms began in 1978, the government planned everything for businesses. Chinese companies had no opportunity to do business with foreign firms and had little international experience in negotiations. This doesn't mean that Chinese businesses are incompetent in this regard. On the contrary, they have their own methods. Confucian principles, Sun Zi's stratagems, and Chinese special circumstances, including government interference, all play a role. For example, to Westerners, negotiation is the time to complete the deal, but to the Chinese it is an ongoing process since *guanxi* is a long-term charge and things can always change. It may be too reckless to let a contract bring everything to its conclusion. It is just as Ming-Jer Chen said in *Inside Chinese Business,* "Chinese negotiations have a beginning, a middle, but no end."

The terms to be negotiated play a vital role. Generally speaking, there are two types of deal that involve negotiation: goods and services. Since goods are tangible, it is relatively straightforward to calculate labor cost and shipment expenses. Both sides may find it easier to understand what is being discussed at the negotiation table. Services are a different story. Service businesses are still not popular in China even today. A large number of business owners and managers don't really understand the logic of paying a business for research and consultation. They would rather get such services for free or in exchange for their recommendations to do a type of business they can understand. On the other hand, it is difficult to calculate the price for services since the costs appear too intangible. So if you come to China to negotiate a service contract, be prepared to find it more challenging.

These conceptual and cultural differences mean that, in the eyes of the Chinese, Western businessmen are too impatient, impersonal, and aggressive, wanting to have the contract sewn up within one day to begin making profits the next morning. On the other hand, Westerners view their Chinese counterparts as hospitable hosts but shrewd negotiators with skillful bargaining stratagems. These differences may easily turn negotiation into misunderstanding, resulting in distrust and failure to reach an agreement. Our advice below and in the next chapter is aimed at avoiding this situation.

NEGOTIATION TEAMS: OLD CHINA AND NEW CHINA

You will likely meet two broad types of Chinese at the negotiation table. The first are old-fashioned officials from government agencies and large SOEs. Most of them are in their 40s and 50s. They are generally conservative in manner and traditional in approach. With this old type of Chinese, you need to be fully prepared and very patient. Try not to appear arrogant and haughty for they have a strong sense of face value and expect your due respect. In their eyes, individualism, candor, directness, assertiveness, and straightforwardness, the values celebrated in the West, are not practical at all. Modesty and humility are what to expect.

The second are well-educated young people who have received training in negotiation, team management, and the business process. They are usually very structural and specifics-oriented with the goal of signing the contract and making profits as soon as possible. If you negotiate with the second type, you can be more relaxed and more yourself. Nevertheless, people from this group are generally too young to be key players. If they tell you that their company is very international, you should be more at ease. But if they hint that their boss is quite conservative, you may come across an opaque decision-making structure where somebody from the first group still needs to give the nod to the final version.

Generally speaking, the Chinese team is composed of the person in charge of the project under discussion, technical personnel, and an interpreter. All will play an important role, but the person who has the final say about the terms and conditions of the contract usually does not takes part in the negotiation process. You may have a chance to meet him at the welcome banquet before the start of the process and at the ceremony when the contract is signed. With a large-scale and complicated project, more government departments may be involved in the approval process and more time will be needed.

No matter what type of people you will deal with, you should be fully prepared. When you provide the names and titles of all your team, you should ask for similar information from the Chinese side and try your best to know their background. If possible, locate the real person or persons in power, most likely through *guanxi* networks.

PRE-NEGOTIATION: BUILDING TRUST

For most Western businessmen, the focus of negotiation is to sit down and review a proposed deal item by item. However, to most Chinese, getting to know who is sitting on the opposite side of the table is more important than the negotiation itself, especially in the initial stages. In other words, the *guanxi* network must be established before talking about business. If you feel confused or get a bit lost here, please go back and read the chapter on *guanxi*.

CASE STUDY

Hospitable host meets eager businessmen

Attracted by the market in China, Bob, the owner of an American company, participated in an Oregon business delegation to Fujian province, the state's sister province in southern China. The delegation would stay in Fujian for one week and make initial overtures to discuss business potential and cooperation. This was Bob's first time in China and he was eager to use this trip as a platform to develop his business in the Chinese market. At first, he was quite impressed by the hospitality of their Chinese host. At the airport they were met by several government officials and taken by limousine to a luxury hotel. The next day, they were introduced to the provincial leaders and then heads of local import and export companies, although Bob had a feeling that these meetings were more symbolic than substantial.

After the initial meetings, the host took the delegation on sightseeing trips and to traditional Chinese shows. The schedule for the delegation was full, with one banquet after another, but nothing was directly related to business deals. Some members hinted to the host that they hoped to sit down and talk about business. But the Chinese host seemed indifferent to this; instead, they kept talking about friendship and sister-province relationship. It was not until the last day of the trip that the Chinese side finally sat down with them, talking about business potential and showing some product samples. On his way back to Oregon, Bob was very disappointed. He came back home empty handed, without any expected business contracts except making some Chinese acquaintances.

Bob's disappointment and confusion are understandable. To him and most Westerners, business is business rather than people and relationships. If one company wants to sell its product or services, what it needs to do is to find the most effective way to reach the target market and convince clients about its services or products. Better service, competitive pricing, and quality products are what attract and retain customers. Free sightseeing trips and frequent dinners are not necessary at all. In addition, time is money. Business negotiations mingled with sightseeing and entertainment is a waste of time and money. As for good *guanxi* and relationships, they are by-products of a successful business deal rather than the other way around.

However, to most Chinese, business should be conducted on the basis of mutual trust, since it is the people who do business and it is the *guanxi* that endures. During these seemingly non-business-related events, the Chinese side tries to gain an understanding of you as a person, seeks to judge if your company can be a trustworthy partner, and decides if you can make a long-term commitment. They are interested in your personal side; they want to know your background, your family, your likes and dislikes, and so on. At the same time, they also expect you to be interested in getting to know them as a human being rather than as just a business partner. The Chinese are more likely to cooperate and make concessions later at the negotiation table to those who are willing to continue *guanxi*. In the case presented above, what Bob gained at the end of the trip is actually very precious for his future business development in China: a *guanxi* network. If he could continue and cultivate this *guanxi* after returning to the US, he would harvest the fruits on his future trips to China.

If you go to China for business negotiations, you may have similar experiences. Don't repeat Bob's mistake. Before your trip, you should plan a longer and more flexible stay in China compared to similar trips to other countries. When invited to attend entertainment activities, you should gladly accept the invitation and return this hospitality in one way or another. In the meantime, enjoy yourself with the gourmet Chinese food, places of historical interest, beauty spots, traditional Chinese performances, and of course, informal conversations through which you can get to know your business partner better. Even if you feel frustrated at the endless, time-consuming, and non-business-related process, you should exercise patience.

NEGOTIATION: KEEPING THE BALL ROLLING

Starting Negotiations

Business negotiations usually take place in a conference room with an oval, round, or rectangular table in the middle. The two negotiation teams sit opposite to each other, with the heads of the delegations sitting in the middle, eye to eye. The interpreters usually sit next to the host and main

Can you tell which side is the guest delegation?

guest. The guest delegation is seated facing the door. The leader of the Chinese side should come into the room first and sit in the middle or wait at the entrance of the conference room with the rest of the team standing behind or next to the head according to their rank. You will be introduced to the Chinese head first and then the team members shake hands all round. The Chinese side will then show you to your seat. You should try to learn the names of your Chinese counterparts before the meeting. When being introduced to each other, you should first shake hands with the person being introduced, nod slightly, and then carefully exchange business cards (refer to the previous chapter for the ritual of business card exchange).

Deal Presentation

A serious negotiation meeting starts with some small talk in order to get the ball rolling. The head of the host team delivers a short welcoming speech and then the head of the guest team follows suit. In your speech, you should introduce the background of your company, including anything notable that has been achieved in a non-boasting way: how your company is organized, what products you make, where you market and sell them, whether your company has partnerships with well-known international companies and government agencies, how you see your company's future in relation to its Chinese counterpart, and what your company can do to make the business deal beneficial to both sides. In the speech, please always stress that the benefits are mutual. You need to conclude your speech by asking your counterpart about their hopes for this potential cooperation. This will lead your Chinese counterpart nicely into their introduction and expectation from this deal. In the subsequent presentation and intercourse with your counterpart, try to speak slowly, clearly, concisely, and carefully. Avoid using acronyms, jargon, idioms, or slang. All members of your delegation should remain polite and cooperative throughout.

Tough Items to Negotiate

Price—Price is the key element of any business negotiation. And the Chinese are particularly well known for being price-sensitive. This is due to China's history of economic and political instability, which meant its people had to save money for times of adversity. They aim to buy goods that are *Wu Mei Jia Lian* (high quality at a lower price). Because of this tradition, the Chinese negotiating team may bargain a great deal over price, usually through haggling. You may find that they will leave less room to maneuver than most Westerners are used to, and make concessions with great reluctance. There is a joke about the business negotiation culture in China: When a Westerner leaves for home at the end of the negotiation, he would say "Have a good evening," while a Chinese business person would say, "Please lower the price for us tomorrow morning."

To reduce the price to the lowest possible point, the Chinese side may prolong the process to exhaust your patience or make you aware of the long-term benefits you may have in exchange for the lower price. In such a situation, we suggest that you give the best price you can to your Chinese partner. China is a very large market that attracts almost all the businesses in the world. If you are unwilling to give a better price, your competitors will. Your willingness to compromise may open a wider door for your business expansion in the country. Also, the Chinese value long-term relationships and will not forget the favor received. They will find a way to return it, for example, by looking for other good business opportunities in China for you or share their experience on how to avoid some possible pitfalls. All these cannot be bought with money but can be vital to your business success. At the same time, to make up for the loss caused by the lower price you give to the Chinese side, you can request more favorable terms in other areas, for example, a larger purchase order, a faster delivery time, quality guarantee, favorable payment terms or conditions, to name a few.

FYI

Chinese price sensitivity has been a headache for many multinational companies operating in China. For example, only white-collar workers of multinational companies can afford to buy from IKEA, while in the US IKEA's target market aims at low-income, apartment dwellers, and college students. To open up a larger market, IKEA has taken every means to reduce prices to a level that more Chinese can afford or accept psychologically, by cutting profit margins, selling more local goods, and using cheap local labor. Other companies, such as Proctor and Gamble, sell a smaller portion of their products than in the Western market to attract more buyers.

On the other hand, after 30 years of economic reforms, the consumption concept of Chinese people has changed dramatically. China now has a small number of wealthy people who are no longer price sensitive but sport brand names and lead luxurious lifestyles. To maintain economic growth, the government has taken measures to encourage ordinary people to spend rather than to put money away in the bank. These measures include lowering bank interest rates, giving longer holidays, and providing favorable terms for housing loans. Most important of all, people have been introduced to a new consumption concept: *"Xing jia bi,"* meaning that people should buy products with the optimal performance/price ratio. This term has become very popular and has greatly influenced people's consumption behavior.

Equity Share and Management Control—If the deal is about a joint venture option, the most sensitive issues would be the percentage of equity holding for each side and management control. The Chinese side generally insists on at least a 50% share and believes that a larger ownership will lead to their control of the newly restructured company. It is also a matter of state sovereignty and national face. In a documentary film on Haier, the largest electronic manufacturer in China, there is an episode in which the Haier side declined a very attractive offer from an American company because the latter insisted on a 51% ownership share. Here we share another real case.

CASE STUDY

Kodak's choice: market share or equity share?

In the late 1990s, Kodak successfully acquired six out of seven Chinese film manufacturers with the support of the Chinese government. The one remaining company was always a headache for Kodak, which could not get the full support of the government. At the same time, Fuji, another world giant in the film production sector, contacted the Chinese company to form a joint venture in order to compete against Kodak in the Chinese market. In 2003, to everyone's surprise, Kodak signed a contract with the Chinese company, agreeing to the Chinese side owning an 80% equity share and having management control of the new joint venture. It was said that the reason Kodak won the deal over Fuji is that the latter insisted on the majority equity share.

SIGNING THE CONTRACT AND THEREAFTER

After a series of talks at the negotiation table mixed with arguing, bargaining, explaining, and defending each side's standpoints, interests, and legal provisions, a contract is signed, indicating a successful completion of the negotiation cycle. To Westerners, a signed contract is a legal document that binds all parties involved and leaves little room for changes to the advantage of any party. What follows is the implementation of the contract. To the Chinese, however, a contract may carry a somewhat different meaning.

A contract brings both sides to a new platform of the *guanxi* relationship, binding the two parties together rather than representing a pamphlet of terms and conditions. To many Chinese, a signed contract is just an agreement between the two parties and the terms should be open for further discussion if the situation changes. It is therefore possible that you will be asked again to lower the price at the airport when leaving for home with the signed contract in your briefcase or perhaps pay a training cost that the Chinese side has already agreed to pay in the contract. Such differing attitudes towards the role and authority of the legal contract are another source of frustration to foreign businesses.

We can trace the general attitude of the Chinese towards law to the Confucian tradition, which puts a greater value on people's self-cultivation and group cohesion rather than relying on legal documents. As Pye summarized, the American secure an agreement or a contract on the basis of a "stable and enduring legal system" while for the Chinese a contract establishes a sort of personal relationship and its security lies in "the strength of human relationship ... [and] a philosophy that governance is more by people than by law" (Pye 1986, 79).

The macro business environment of China also plays a role in the general attitude of the Chinese toward legal documents like contracts. China developed its economy in a way that no other country has, so there are no prior experience that can be applied. Methodology is always subject to change, including laws, regulations, and policies. Let us look at what Vincent Lo said and did about this.

CASE STUDY

Chinese and Western views on contract are as different as the languages they speak

Vincent Lo is the Chairman of Shui On Group. His success in building Xintiandi in Shanghai made him well known worldwide. In an interview, he mentioned that at the completion of negotiations for constructing the billion-dollar Xintiandi project, the contract amounted to only four pages. He said: "It's the local way to view the contract since people cannot predict everything in the contract; on the contrary, people should change the terms as the situation changes. There is a Chinese saying 'Planning can never catch up with changes.' " It indicates how flexible the Chinese are and how ready they are for changes. That's why the Chinese and Westerners hold different views about contracts.

It will cause you a lot of inconvenience and frustration if a contract cannot be implemented due to change or government interference (Child 2006).

But according to the research of Ghauri and Fang (2001), Chinese businesses have generally honored contracts. Remember that the Chinese value their face and long-term *guanxi* based on mutual trust.

To you, a Western business person, it is still important to maintain a good relationship with your Chinese partner, even though the contract has been signed. They may help sidestep possible bureaucratic and government interference. It is even better if you have your own government *guanxi* that can help settle any contractual dispute due to a changed situation or other interference.

Over the three decades of implementing the open-door policy and economic reforms, the Chinese government has established its legal system and enforcement mechanism. The Chinese now have cultivated a much sharper sense of the law pertaining to legal documents like contracts. This is especially the case in the better-developed areas, such as Shanghai, Beijing, and Shenzhen. In the new phase of the economic reforms, more and more leading Chinese corporations are expanding their business in international markets through mergers and acquisitions, building factories overseas, and going public on the Hong Kong and US stock markets. Chinese businesses are learning to conform to international norms and rules, although many other companies still hold fast to traditional notions in regards to contracts.

12 Behind the Negotiation Table (II)

I n this chapter we explore in more depth some of the issues brought up in the previous chapter. We focus on the negotiation stratagems reportedly used by the Chinese, summarize the problems foreign businesses may come across in China due to cultural influence and organizational restraints, and suggest ways to achieve optimal results for your efforts.

MIND GAMES IN NEGOTIATION

The Chinese value relationship and face, but they are also internationally known as shrewd, skillful, tough, and tenacious negotiators (Ghauri and Fang 2001). As discussed in Chapters 4 and 5 on understanding the Chinese mentality, Confucianism teaches the Chinese to avoid confrontation with each other while Sun Zi's *The Art of War* and *The Thirty-Six Stratagems* provide a set of soft strategies to win the battle without fighting. The combination of these two compounded with China's social, legal, economic, and technological macros has shaped the way in which the Chinese conduct business negotiations with foreign companies. The following is a summary of the negotiation strategies based on published research, for example, Pye (1982, 1994) and Fang (1999).

Another Aspect of *Guanxi*

As discussed in the chapter on *guanxi*, the stronger party has more obligations to the weaker one, as in a family where the oldest sibling has to take care of the younger ones. Most books on Chinese negotiation style mention that Chinese negotiators love to take advantage of their weakness in technology or lack of capital and turn such weakness into an advantage in negotiations. During negotiations, the Chinese side might flatter you and your company excessively and describe you as a powerful giant in the global market with the hope that you will make more concessions. If this happens, you can find a middle path between making concessions and sticking to your principles by asking the Chinese side to compromise in other areas and make the deal a win-win situation for both parties.

You could also show your interest in the Chinese market in general or the local market in particular and seek their opinions or suggestions about how to better respond to local situations in terms of politics, economy, consumption trends, or unique local culture. By doing so, you can turn yourself into a weaker player. The Chinese side will love to see you soften your attitude and be willing to offer a helping hand.

Home Court Advantage

Your Chinese counterparts may suggest that negotiations take place in China rather than in your home country. Most books call this tactic the "Home Court Advantage." It means that the Chinese side can take advantage of familiar surroundings, people, laws and regulations, and government. This corresponds to Sun Zi's strategy for winning a war: right time, right place, and right people ("*Tianshi dili renhe*"). This strategy is especially vital if we consider the fact that China still lacks full transparency in its administrative processes and is short of a complete set of business laws. When a ready answer cannot be found in laws and regulations, your Chinese counterpart may refer to internal regulations. This may put you at a disadvantage since you are in the dark over these rules. In these circumstances you should hire a reliable local intermediary or hire a good Chinese lawyer.

Another disadvantage you may have if negotiations are held in China is that over time you may lose control, especially if you have deadline pressure, since nobody wants to go home empty handed. Therefore, you should always plan to stay longer on your business trips to China than you would for other countries.

Good Cop–Bad Cop

"Good cop–bad cop" is another tactic often used by Chinese negotiators. To do this, the Chinese delegates are usually divided into teams: good cops who play softball and bad cops who play hardball, allowing more flexibility and the ability to alternate strategies during negotiations. A Chinese MBA student who used to be a business representative for a Chinese import and export corporation shared the following experience with us:

> Before we would leave for a negotiation meeting, we would decide between ourselves who would play the good cop and who would play the bad cop. We would prepare two sets of prices, for example, one being about 10% to 20% higher than the other. During negotiations, the bad cop always talks first to test the water. He would quote the first set of prices, telling the other side that this is the best we can do. If the other side shows an interest, we move on to other issues, such as quality control or the date of shipment. If they don't show any interest or express difficulty in accepting the offer, the good cop starts to talk. He would suggest that they should not give up yet since the price is negotiable after consulting superiors. The good cop may also suggest having dinner together. In the middle of the dinner, when everybody forgets the negotiations, the good cop again brings business back into the conversation. Then the bad cop begins to reinforce the viewpoints stated at the negotiation table. If the other side still does not give in, the good cop would often position himself to speak on behalf of the other side and try to persuade the bad cop to give a better quote or condition. The negotiations go back and forth in this way before an agreement is reached.

Many Chinese know about and can use the good cop and bad cop strategy in their daily life. For example, when Chinese parents teach their children at home, mother usually plays the role of the good cop and father the bad cop. As the bad cop, the father sets up the rules and punishes the child who disobeys. As a good cop, the mother softens the blow by explaining to the child why the father has to punish him. This strategy can effectively discipline children without letting them feel isolated and abandoned by their parents.

However, the good cop and bad cop strategy is more often used with new business partners. To an established customer, the Chinese are more direct and to the point because both sides have set up a mutually dependent relationship already.

Testing the Bottom Line

Some Western business people have observed that their Chinese hosts sometimes go out with them for entertainment, but do not necessarily separate business from pleasure. They seem to work harder at the dinner table than at the negotiation table. While eating, they try to find out background information and the full intention of their counterpart's trip, their bottom-line price for the products they intend to buy, and so on. By doing this, the Chinese negotiators can be better prepared and gain an edge over their counterparts. This kind of practice is called *mo di* in Chinese, which means "testing the bottom." One American friend jokingly told us that by *mo di* at a dinner banquet, the Chinese side simply changes its "battlefield" from the negotiation table to the dinner table. It is another Sun Zi-like stratagem.

More about Stratagems

By now you may be confused about why Chinese negotiators sometimes act as Confucian gentlemen and at other times behave like a Sun Zi-type strategist. It is always hard to tell when they are Confucian gentlemen and when they are skillful strategists. But we believe when you have established a good *guanxi*, the Chinese negotiators will act more like gentlemen. However, when mutual trust is low, the same person may play the game using more of the above-mentioned stratagems. If this happens more than you can tolerate, you need to examine yourself in terms of relationship cultivation with your Chinese counterpart or reconsider another Chinese partner, since there may be too big a gap between you and the current partner.

SOME ISSUES YOU MAY OVERLOOK

Lack of Global Business Experience

One of Sun Zi's most popular quotations is: "Know yourself and know your opponent; you will be invincible." China is a relatively new player in the global market and will need time to accumulate experience, knowledge, and business professionalism when doing business with foreign companies. This may sometimes give the Chinese a feeling of insecurity and vulnerability as they are not yet familiar with certain aspects of their counterparts.

FYI

As discussed in Chapter 2, China began its open-door policy and internal reforms in the late 1970s. Since then, Western theories on management, marketing, international trade, and negotiation have begun to be introduced into Chinese business circles. This can be seen in the Chinese language itself which has incorporated many new terms in recent years to refer to new business concepts, such as "private equity," "reinsurance," and "mergers and acquisitions."

CASE STUDY

Mergers and acquisitions: a new concept in China

A Wharton MBA told us a story. He was once representing his firm as part of a consulting team for a Chinese company that intended to acquire a sector of a large foreign company. The Chinese company planned to enter the international market through the deal, while the foreign company wanted to sell its unprofitable sector for restructuring purposes. Several other companies were also interested in acquiring the foreign company's unprofitable sector. Since mergers and acquisitions were so new to the Chinese side, the consulting team spent a great deal of time explaining the basic meaning of mergers and acquisitions to the management level of the Chinese company and officials from the local government, as well as outlining the advantages, disadvantages, risks, and potentials. It was a hard process since the Chinese side was reluctant to accept the fact that they had to increase the offer price to beat their competitors. The deal failed in the end.

As a negotiator, you may from time to time sense feelings of insecurity on the Chinese side due to their lack of knowledge. The Chinese use tactics with which they protect themselves from disadvantages. They may emphasize their advantages, such as a large market and potential long-term cooperation. They will receive you with special treatment and make you feel obligated to take care of them as *guanxi* insiders. Another tactic could be to prolong the negotiation process in order not to make errors and avoid being taken advantage of. So you may hear responses like, "We will discuss this matter next time" or "We need to consult people in other departments." To show your goodwill, you can offer to share your own experience of doing business in the global market. The Chinese side will definitely appreciate it.

Lack of Efficiency

In the course of negotiations, you may feel frustrated by the inconsistency or inefficiency on the part of the Chinese side. It should come as no surprise if you are told that you need to discuss something that was agreed upon two months ago or even just the day before. Please bear in mind that China is developing fast. Something that was not an issue a couple of years ago may now be a serious problem that needs immediate attention or quick solution. For instance, parking in metropolitan areas was not an issue several years ago. But nowadays, when designing a new community, parking has become a real headache since new regulations stipulate that parking lots must be built in every new community. This increases the cost and reduces the building area. So there is always the possibility that some new government policy may impede the smooth running of the negotiation process.

There is also the possibility that the negotiation team has no power to make a final decision on the deal. They gather the information and report to the people at the upper level, often perhaps consulting with several departments. More often than not, the real decision makers may know little about the technical details and the technical people have to spend a long time explaining and convincing them to accept what has been proposed.

Because of the lack of international experience, the Chinese tend to discuss principles rather than details at the negotiation table in order to gain themselves enough leeway, especially so when the decision makers know little about the core of the deal. This is another reason why negotiations with the Chinese can stretch longer than expected. Hence you have to be very patient and tolerant, and plan on staying longer to give yourself and your Chinese partner time to finish negotiations.

Language Issues at the Negotiation Table

Sometimes you may find it difficult to grasp the true intention of the Chinese side, even though you know perfectly well what they say on the surface. You may also find that they use unconvincing data to support their argument. One reason is that the Chinese like to speak in a circular way rather than directly, using many allusions and anecdotes that you are not familiar with. So the importance of finding a qualified interpreter cannot be more emphasized. He or she must be someone who can not only translate the literal meaning but the connotations hidden behind the phrases. Other than that, the interpreter should understand the basics of the technology involved and know the technical terms. Before the process begins, ask your interpreter to read relevant documents as a preparation. When you speak, articulate yourself concisely, clearly, and slowly and leave some room for the interpreter to translate into Chinese. If you find gaps in understanding the other side through translation, check with the interpreter about what is being said.

National Pride

As discussed in the section about face, the Chinese are very sensitive about "national face" or "national pride" when dealing with foreigners. As somebody from the Western world, you need to watch your attitude. Please don't show that your country is better and more advanced than China. Avoid criticizing China for its inefficiency or corrupt officials. You can never force your Chinese opponents to accept your position during negotiation simply because you know the international rules or own more advanced technology. It may backfire and ruin your business prospects.

CASE STUDY

You'll pay the price if you look down upon your Chinese partner

A foreign company negotiated with a Chinese government delegation. The former wanted to sell the latter a sewing machine factory that produced out-of-date machines. The price was reasonable and there was potentially a huge market for that type of sewing machine in rural China. Both sides reached a basic agreement. Then a representative of the foreign company looked triumphant and implied by his tone that the Chinese wanted to buy their junk. The next day the Chinese side announced that they had changed their mind because they wanted to buy more up-to-date equipment.

The Chinese dislike people who put on airs and show off their strength. They want to be treated on an equal footing despite their technological disadvantages and lack of knowledge on new business concepts. They do not want to do business with people who look down upon the Chinese and China. Such a hurt to their national pride will definitely result in failure for any business deal.

MORE TIPS FOR SUCCESS

Be Courteous

At the negotiation table, the Chinese tend to humble themselves while flattering you: "We have much to learn from you because our work in the field is very backward" or "This is our first meeting, please advise whenever possible." This is a Chinese way to maintain harmony and give face to you as a foreign guest. Be careful not to show your superiority. Instead you should express that you have much to learn from the Chinese side as well and that the success of the business deal will benefit both sides. Being modest is a Chinese tradition and you are expected to display the same.

Be Careful When Saying "No"

In order to maintain harmony and save face, the Chinese tend to avoid confrontation. If they disagree with you, they may keep silent, or defer by saying that they will report to a superior or discuss it later. In this situation you should be patient, since the Chinese side will consider the issue and come back with a counter-offer. If you are not happy with something raised at the table, you should be cautious about giving an honest "No." You could keep silent and look for another opportunity to bring up the matter in an indirect manner. Or you could make concessions on other terms but insist on this as a pre-condition.

Silence is an indirect way of saying "No" in Chinese culture. If you find the Chinese side suddenly becomes quiet and stops negotiating, it indicates that they disagree with you or do not want to respond to your request. When silence falls at the negotiation table, do not feel you have to say something. You can sit quietly, waiting, looking sideways, or raising a different point. Any unsolved issues can be taken care of at another time if you can raise them in a more tactful way.

Know the Team

As already mentioned in the previous chapter, before starting business negotiations, you need to provide a list of your negotiation team to your Chinese counterpart. The list should be arranged in order of seniority or importance in relation to the negotiated deal. You should ask for a similar list from the Chinese side and memorize the names and titles, especially the people who have the authority to make decisions.

Send People with Title and Power

Chinese culture values what age brings to the business deal. Age is another name for wisdom, experience, and even power. Rank and title of the negotiators indicate the importance your company has attached to the proposed deal. With this in mind, you ought to send an older person with the highest possible position as head of the negotiating team. In return, the Chinese side will have an equally powerful person in the team to show their respect. With a more powerful person on the Chinese side, your negotiations may quickly come to a close since the leader of the team can make a quick decision or even make a decision on the spot. This decision-making person may not know much about the technological aspects of the deal and so may ignore many details. This will bring your side a better chance of winning.

Be Patient

It takes time to get business done in China, so patience with your Chinese counterparts is very important. It's always wise to lay out your basic position at this time. You'll find it very useful to distribute sheets stating your main points in Chinese. Be very direct and to the point when tackling a business issue. You should speak carefully and try to quote correct figures at the negotiation table as your Chinese counterpart may take careful notes and quote your own words to refute your position at a later stage in the negotiation process. At some point, you may not be clear about what the Chinese side really wants. Be patient and cautious about what you reveal at the negotiation table.

Facts Speak Louder than Words

To convince the Chinese side to accept your terms, you can try the following:

1. Clearly explain the input and output, effort and gain, short-term and long-term aspects of the deal with the help of figures and examples.
2. In general, Chinese people don't like anyone talking too much. It is more convincing to present the facts objectively without interweaving too much subjective feeling.
3. Move your counterparts with emotion and show them your sincerity by approaching the issue under discussion from the Chinese perspective and considering their situation, difficulty, and interests. Your consideration and care will be a sign of friendship and lead to a successful completion of the negotiations.

13 Eating and Drinking Your Way to Success

From the previous chapters, you have learned that the quality and quantity of *guanxi* and the tactful use of face are vital to your business success in China. You have also learned that a dinner table is a crucial place to start, develop, and consolidate the relationship. To help you perform well, this chapter gives an introduction to the basics of the various styles of Chinese cuisines and highlights some important dining and drinking etiquette. This knowledge will help you appreciate Chinese culture in the presence of your host, giving you an edge in building a *guanxi* network and helping you move towards your business goal.

PRINCIPLES OF CHINESE CUISINES

Almost everybody loves to eat but the Chinese seem to love it more, with common greetings such as, "Have you eaten?" and "What did you eat last night?" It is no wonder that China has some of the world's greatest food, from market-stall buns to the intricate variations of regional cuisines. When you are in China, don't miss any dining opportunities presented to you. As one American businessman put it, "If you can't get business done in China, that's your company's loss, but if you don't enjoy and appreciate the delectable and authentic food in China, that's your loss."

The principles of Chinese cuisine are closely related to the Daoist beliefs on *yin* and *yang*. Everything in the universe is either positive or negative, wet or dry, cold or hot, light or dark, male or female, plus or minus. This applies to what we eat: meat, fowl, vegetable, fruit, nuts, and liquid. *Yin* foods are thin, bland, cooling, and low in calories while *yang* foods are rich, spicy, warming, and high in calories. Boiling will make food *yin* while deep-frying makes food *yang*.

Likewise, each individual is constitutionally *yin* or *yang* or a combination of the two, categorized as "positive," "negative," and "nervous" respectively. If a human being is to remain right with the cosmos, he should harmonize these opposing forces in order to be sound and healthy. For example, if you become "wet" or "cold" temporarily due to the weather or for health reasons, you should eat something "dry" or "hot" to regain balance within yourself.

The Chinese also believe that different flavors have different impacts on one's health. For example, peppery foods can clean the lungs, bitter foods relieve gastroenteritis, sour foods refresh and strengthen the liver, salty foods strengthen the kidneys and bones, and sweet foods invigorate the spleen. The person who arranges the menu for a dinner banquet must keep these principles in mind and consider the features of the dishes available in relation to the health of the people attending the dinner, trying to satisfy everybody with different kinds of dishes. In addition, he needs to take into consideration the look, aroma, touch, taste, nutrition, and even sound effect of the chosen dishes.

Based on the principle of *yin* and *yang* balance, very few Chinese dishes have only one ingredient. Usually there is a main ingredient and a number of supplementary ingredients. Take pork for example: its color is pink and its texture tender. It is most likely to be found with a green vegetable that is either crispy or crunchy, such as celery or green peppers. The concept of harmonization doesn't stop with individual dishes but is carried through the entire meal. No meal is made up of a single dish; dishes are served in

Yin–Yang emblems

民以食为天

Eating comes first

pairs, fours, sixes, eights, tens, or even more. Similarly, the order in which food is served is dictated by the requirements of harmony. In other words, from the individual dishes to the sequence of serving, the meal must be harmonious.

ONE CHINA, MANY CUISINES

China is so vast that each region has its own unique local cuisine. Generally speaking, northern dishes are strongly flavored with onions or garlic, while eastern food is more delicate and lightly spiced with a hint of onion or ginger. The exception is the city of Wuxi, where sweetness can overwhelm other flavors, or Shanghai, where dishes can be very oily. The western-China food from Sichuan or Hunan can be dominated by the strong flavor of brown peppercorn and chillies, while southerners prefer complex, subtle sauces that accentuate the fresh flavors of the ingredients. Even the same ingredient can differ widely across the country. In olden times, traveling merchants from Shanxi Province carried jugs of Shanxi vinegar with them rather than use what they considered the inferior sourness of other vinegars.

In general, Chinese food is roughly divided into eight regional cuisines, with the best-known being Sichuan, Shandong, and Guangdong. Beijing and Shanghai cuisines are just as popular, so they are included in the following list arranged in alphabetical order. In addition, Appendix H lists some typical dishes from each of the regional cuisines together with Chinese pinyin pronunciation, which should help you order food by yourself.

Anhui Cuisine

Hui Cai or Anhui cooking preserves most of the original taste and nutrition of the ingredients. The food is usually slightly spicy and salty. Some master dishes are stewed in brown sauce with heavy stress on oil and the sauce. Ham is often added to improve the taste and the addition of sugar achieves freshness. Typical courses are Huangshan braised pigeon, hot diced pork, Wuwei smoked duck, stewed soft shell turtle with ham, steamed stone frog, steamed rock partridge, stewed fish belly in brown sauce, and bamboo shoots cooked with sausage and dried mushroom.

Beijing Cuisine

Gongting Cai or imperial cuisine from Beijing has combined many features of other local cuisines, especially the Shandong cuisine. Typical dishes include Beijing roast duck, instant-boiled mutton, Mongolian hot pot, braised shark's fin, and sweet cakes with dates.

Beijing roast duck is widely known as a most delicious dish. Eating it is regarded as one of the two must-do's while in the city. The other is climbing the Great Wall. Beijing roast duck is made by stuffing the duck with minced sheep's tripe, parsley, spring onion, and salt before heating it in an oven over flames of fruit-tree wood or charcoal fire. The two most famous restaurants for the dish are Bianyifang Roast Duck Restaurant and Quanjude Roast Duck Restaurant, representing two different styles of roasting duck and both with a history of over one hundred years.

The chef comes to your table to show you the whole roasted duck, which he then cuts at your table into roughly 120 pieces, both the skin and the meat. The duck is served with special pancakes, hollowed sesame buns, green onions, and sweet soybean paste. The waiter or waitress will teach you how to wrap all of these into a small roll inside the pancake. People often include sliced garlic and cucumber as well. Some parts of the duck will be served either as cold dishes, such as the liver, wings, stomach, webs, and eggs, or hot dishes with fried heart, tongue, and kidneys. The duck bone is boiled into a soup as the final dish of the dinner. Because of

Beijing's roast duck's excellent taste and famous name, KFC in China has begun to offer a similar dish but using chicken instead.

Fujian Cuisine

Min Cai is the cuisine of Fujian and consists of several varieties: Fuzhou Cuisine, Quanzhou Cuisine, and Xiamen Cuisine. It is recognized for its seafood, beautiful color, and the magic tastes of sweet, sour, salty, and savory. The most characteristic aspect of Fujian cuisine is that most dishes are served in a soup. The most famous dish is called *Fo Tiao Qiang* (Buddha Jumps Over the Wall). The name implies that the dish is so delicious that even a monk would jump over a wall to eat it once he smells it. Others include Snow Chicken and Prawn with Dragon's Body and Phoenix's tail—dragon and phoenix are fanciful names for snake and chicken. A mixture of seafood, chicken, duck, and pork is put into a rice-wine jar and simmered over a low fire. Quick-boiled sea mussels in chicken soup is another Fujian delicacy.

Guangdong Cuisine

Yue Cai or Cantonese food is perhaps the most widely available Chinese cuisine outside China since the majority of overseas Chinese are from Guangdong. Guangdong cuisine is usually clear, light, crisp, and fresh. Steaming and stir-frying are the most–commonly used cooking techniques for preserving the natural flavors. Guangdong chefs also attend to the artistic presentation of dishes. Typical dishes are shark's fin soup, steamed sea bass, roast piglet, sizzling beef, and sweet and sour pork. Other famous dishes are dragon, tiger, and phoenix with chrysanthemum (snake, cat, and chicken), braised phoenix liver and snake slices (chicken liver and snake), and stir-fried shredded snake meat in five colors. The most famous dish, Dragon and Tiger Fight, is a dish of braised snake and cat.

FYI

The Cantonese are widely known for their adventurous palate, eating many different kinds of meats and vegetables. In fact, people in northern China often say that Cantonese people can eat anything that flies except airplanes, anything that moves on the ground except trains and cars, and anything that moves in the water except boats. This is of course an overstatement.

Hunan Cuisine

Xiang Cai or Hunan cuisine is similar in flavor to Sichuan cuisine, but spicier and with a larger variety of ingredients. Hunan is very humid, so the local people eat more hot peppers to help remove dampness and cold. Typical courses are Dong'an Chick, peppery and hot chick, and lotus seedpods with crystal sugar.

Jiangsu Cuisine

Jiangsu cuisine, shortened as *Su Cai,* is also called Huaiyang cuisine. Known in China as a land of fish and rice, Jiangsu has a rich variety of seafood as the main ingredients and can be classified into Suzhou–Wuxi style and Zhenjiang–Yangzhou style. Typical dishes are stewed crab with clear soup, long-boiled and dry-shredded meat, salted dried duck (Nanjing's most famous dish), crystal meat (pigs' trotters in a light, brown sauce), Yangzhou steamed jerky strips (dried tofu, chicken, ham, and pea leaves), and Farewell My Concubine (soft-shelled turtle stewed with many other ingredients, such as chicken, mushrooms, and wine).

Shandong Cuisine

Lu Cai or Shandong cuisine is characterized by its aroma, freshness, crispness, and tenderness. Shallots and garlic are used as seasonings, so Shandong dishes usually taste pungent. Soups are given much emphasis. Typical dishes include sea cucumber with meatballs, braised shark's fin with shredded chicken, sea cucumber with mushrooms and bamboo shoots, clams in egg white, fried oysters with trumpet shell braised in soy sauce, sweet and sour carp, Dezhou stewed chicken, caramelized apples, bird's nest soup, which is made from the nests of swiftlets, a tiny bird found throughout Southeast Asia.

Shanghai Cuisine

Hu Cai is Shanghai's cuisine known for its use of alcohol. Fish, eel, crab, and chicken are "drunken" with spirits and then briskly cooked or served raw. The use of sugar is common, usually in combination with soy sauce and other sauces. The taste is savory rather than sweet. The most notable dishes include sweet and sour spare ribs, hot and sour soup with eel and chicken, black sea cucumber with shrimp roe, boiled crucian carp with clam, shrimps of two colors, and steamed beef in rice flour.

Sichuan Cuisine

Chuan Cai is one of the most famous Chinese cuisines in the world and also one of the most popular in China. Characterized by its spicy and pungent flavor, Sichuan cuisine emphasizes the use of chili, pepper, and prickly ash, producing a particular taste called *ma* in Chinese. Besides, garlic, ginger and fermented soybean are also used in the cooking process. Wild vegetables and animals are usually chosen as ingredients. Basic food preparation techniques, such as pickling and braising, are applied. Typical courses are sliced cold chicken, twice cooked pork, shredded pork and hot sauce, hot pot, fish flavored eggplant, and couple's beef fillet.

Zhejiang Cuisine

Zhe Cai is made up of the local cuisines of Hangzhou, Ningbo, and Shaoxing. It is known for its freshness, tenderness, softness, and smoothness together with its mellow fragrance. Hangzhou cuisine is the most famous of the three. Typical dishes are sour West Lake fish, Longjing shelled shrimp, Beggar's Chicken, and Songsao shredded fish soup, which was highly praised by Emperor Qianlong of the Qing Dynasty (1644–1911) as the "Number One Dish in the World!"

Vegetarian Cuisine

Su Cai or vegetarian cuisine is something China is also well known for. Interestingly, a typical menu in a vegetarian restaurant looks the same as a menu in any other restaurant including BBQ pork, mutton curry, fish fillet, fried chicken, and shark's fin soup, however, the dishes contain no meat. Chinese vegetarians believe that the taste, flavor, and texture of meat dishes can be reproduced using non-meat ingredients. The chef selects suitable substitutes and applies different cooking techniques to produce dishes similar in look and taste to dishes using meat. In this way, people can enjoy their favorite food without killing animals. In fact, people unfamiliar with Chinese vegetarian cuisine often do not believe the "chicken" or "beef" they are eating are really vegetarian. You have to try to believe it.

THE CHINESE-STYLE BANQUET

As in a formal Western-styled banquet, a typical Chinese business banquet usually comprises several courses. But different from the Western one that everyone chooses his own drink and eats from his own plate, banquet participants in China share one or two alcoholic drinks but a dozen of common dishes placed on a huge lazy-Susan platform in the center of the table. In other words, you will have little choice with your drinks but can eat a variety of dishes at one meal.

A Chinese banquet starts with an even-numbered selection of cold appetizers. This is followed by a variety of hot main dishes usually presented in a decorative style and consisting of lobster, pork, scallops, and chicken, and often covering the five basic tastes of sweet, sour, salty, spicy, and bitter. A sweet dish is usually served midway through the meal. In some places, soup and rice are the next-to-last dish to be served before a fruit platter. In other places, a banquet ends with a fish dish, which signifies abundance, as the Chinese word for "fish" is a homophone of the Chinese word for "abundance."

Banquet drinks are different from those in the West, where the type of alcohol served matches the meal and the guests' special preferences are accommodated. In China the host often decides on alcoholic beverages for everybody, usually brand-name liquor, wine, and beer. The brand names of Chinese liquor (*baijiu*) include *Shaoxing*, *Wuliangye*, and *Maotai*, the most famous one. This is a potent wine, 55% alcohol content, made from sorghum and often served at important banquets. Each guest has four glasses, one each for water, wine, beer, and liquor.

BANQUETING ETIQUETTE

As discussed earlier, dinner banquets are an important part of Chinese business culture. It is a way to start, develop, and consolidate *guanxi*. An overseas blogger living in China posted the following observation: "Food is important in all cultures, but in China it plays a paramount role as the tool for face and *guanxi*." Chinese hosts show their hospitality, friendship, and respect to foreign business partners through the custom of holding banquets. In addition, a dinner table may be a better place to communicate if some issues and concerns are too difficult or tricky to discuss at the negotiation table. Therefore, as a foreign guest, you should make good use of the opportunities a banquet offers in order to promote friendship and *guanxi*, thereby increasing the chances of a successful business deal. With this aim in mind, we provide a brief summary of Chinese dinner etiquette. Some knowledge of these will help you feel more at ease and gain face for you and your host.

Seating Arrangement

As you already know, the Chinese value rank and title, therefore as invited guests, you should give your host a list of delegation members, their ranks, and titles ahead of time so that the Chinese side will have equivalent people at the dinner table. Seating arrangements are based on rank, age, and title. A round dining table is more often used. The guest of honor is always seated to the right of the principal host; the next in line will sit on his left. This is because traditionally the Chinese regard the right side as superior to the left side. So on formal occasions, including meetings and banquets, the host invariably arranges that the main guest sits on his right side or takes the center seat and everyone else is seated in descending order of status. It is discourteous to seat guests at the place where dishes are served.

Commencing the Banquet

Business banquets are usually held in private rooms of restaurants specially reserved for the purpose. Traditionally, the head of the guest delegation should enter the room first. Sometimes an elaborate ceremony of deference may take place at the door where the most honored guest is escorted to the banquet room by the head of the hosting team. By doing this, the hosting company wants to highlight the guests' importance and respect they have for their guests. As a guest, you should express appreciation for this. Don't be surprised if your hosts greet you with a loud round of applause. The proper response is to applaud back.

The head of the hosting team is the first person to begin the dinner by suggesting the first drink. He will then take the first piece of the most valued food and put it on the guest of honor's plate, as well on the plates of one or two other guests nearby. This gesture signifies the beginning of the meal. Or, the host may simply raise his chopsticks and announce that eating has begun. After this, everybody can start eating.

Toasting

Toasting is always the highlight of a banquet. The first toast is initiated by the head of the hosting team at the beginning of the meal, accompanied by some words of goodwill. When he says "*Ganbei*" (Bottoms up), all present should drain their glasses. After this initial toast, drinking and toasting are open to all. Subsequent toasts can be made from person to person or to the group as a whole. Generally, people on the hosting side take the lead in toasting guests who are seated closest to them. If there is more than one table, the host will go to each table to clink the glass of each individual at the table and then drink a toast to them. Chief guests are expected to follow this custom. It is also a custom for toasts to be proposed between courses, particularly before the mid-meal soup dish. This practice generally has the effect of prolonging the meal and turning it into a noisy party, if it is not a formal banquet.

When giving and receiving toasts, be sure to lift the glass to shoulder height. This is to show utmost respect. When someone toasts you, you should immediately stop eating and drinking to accept and toast in response. If you are far from someone you want to toast, you can use your glass to rap on the table. If there are old people or high-ranking people dining with you, be sure to toast them each at least once. It is advised that when clinking drinks at a party, banquet, or reception, young people and those in lower position should show their respect by clinking the edge of their drinks below the edge of an elder or a high-ranking person.

Serve Others First before Serving Yourself

At a formal banquet, there are waiters or waitresses to help serve the dishes. However, if this is not the case, you should ask people on both sides of you if they would like some of the food and then serve them first before serving yourself. By the same token, your Chinese hosts will always offer to serve food from the central dishes to your plate before serving themselves. The same applies to drinks. Fill the glasses of people sitting next to you before filling your own. You may feel uncomfortable with the rules of Chinese table etiquette, but don't worry, your Chinese hosts generally don't expect you to do much in this respect.

Eating, Drinking, and Face Giving

At a Chinese banquet, it is customary and polite for the host to urge the guest to eat more and drink more and try each and every dish. It's a Chinese way of making sure that you are taken good care of. You may feel some pressure, especially if you are offered something you have never tried before. Be open-minded and try a small piece first to see if you like it or not. If it isn't to your taste, be tactful in letting your host know about this. You can say that you like all the dishes, but this one is a bit beyond you. More often than not, your host will not feel offended since the axiom "one man's meat is another man's poison" is a universal concept. An American businessman shared this story: At a Chinese banquet, he was treated as the most honored guest. When the last course, a fish dish, was served, he was invited to eat the eyes of the fish, a traditional way of the local people to pay respect to the most honored guest at the meal. There was no way he could accept because this part of the fish is never eaten in his culture, so he declined but in a polite and honest way. Along with his excuse, he complimented the food of the day and said that he appreciated the host's generosity. Both sides were happy.

One last thing: never finish all the food on your plate. Otherwise your host might misinterpret this as not having provided enough food, creating a loss of face. Leave a piece of food on your own plate and never take the last piece from the common plates.

The Rules of Drinking

Drinking can be more complicated than eating. Here *ganbei* is perhaps one of the most important words in the Chinese language. You will no doubt hear it a million times during your stay in China. At a banquet, your Chinese host will watch your reaction to the first *ganbei* of the evening and then decide how they are going to drink. If you down your drink on the first one, they will probably expect you to do the same with the follow-up toasts. They may keep urging you to drink more in the belief that the more you drink the closer your relationship with them will become. In some places, getting guests drunk is a matter of courtesy for the host. It indicates that the guests have drunk to their satisfaction. Refusing a drink is normally regarded as impolite and not giving face, therefore it is not worth establishing a friendship or even worth doing business. This is definitely true from one Chinese to another Chinese, but may not be so to foreign businessmen. Here we would like to share with you two real stories.

CASE STUDY

Where there is Maotai, there is business

Tony Wang, an American Chinese, was sent by KFC to China in the late 1980s to open KFC restaurants in Beijing. He drank two bottles of *Maotai* with a group of local government officials before obtaining approval to rent a prime location to start the first KFC store in Beijing. That was the first Western fast-food store opened in China. Thereafter, KFC launched a successful expansion in the country. Definitely, Tony Wang's *Maotai* drink played a role.

CASE STUDY

Face can also be saved without drinking too much Maotai

Another story is about the banquet experience of a foreign businessman in Sichuan. After he drank the first glass of *Maotai*, he felt he could not tolerate it any more. He knew that if he continued drinking the liquor, he would get sick and have to rush to the bathroom, but he would lose face by not drinking more. He instinctively covered the glass with his hand when the waitress came to fill the glass. The head of the Chinese hosts noticed this and ordered the removal of all bottles of *Maotai*. The face of both sides was saved and the banquet continued with a happy tone.

Lightly Sample Each Dish

People not familiar with Chinese banquet meals typically eat too much too soon. In a banquet meal, for example, four appetizer dishes will be served first. But they are not the main courses. Shortly after the appetizer, four more dishes will be served, usually more filling than the first round. Just sample a bite of each since four more dishes—generally the best—will be served soon after. Otherwise, you will have no room for these and feel real pain by the time the last course arrives. Our advice to you is, don't fill

Ganbei (Bottoms up)!

yourself up too soon. You will have more than enough to eat. In addition, it is rude to stop eating in the middle of a banquet and your host may presume that something is wrong with the meal or somebody has offended you. So even if you are full, try a small bite of everything to show your respect. It is acceptable for you to ask what a particular dish is—it's also a good conversation topic at the dinner table.

Give Chopsticks a Chance

Apart from soup, all dishes are eaten with chopsticks at a Chinese dinner table. It will be appreciated if you do the same. The Chinese are particular about the use of chopsticks. Practice manipulating the world's oldest eating utensils and you'll leave a good impression on your host. Even if you don't know how to use chopsticks, at least give it a try before asking for a fork or spoon. Your Chinese host will certainly appreciate your effort and praise you in front of others.

FYI

Confucius (551 BC–479 BC) established the principles for cooking and table etiquette, most of which remain to this day. He reasoned that, as a matter of advancement in civilization, instruments used for killing must be banned from the dining table. Therefore, knives weren't permitted and that is why Chinese food is chopped into bite-sized pieces before it reaches the table. He also advocated the use of chopsticks for this same reason, stating that they reflect gentleness and compassion, the central teaching of Confucianism.

Conversation Topics

There are no firm rules regarding dinner conversation topics. Depending on the closeness of the relationship, business may not be discussed unless the host initiates the topic. Some light topics, such as the arts, food, music, sports, computer games, and the wellbeing of children and family members are safe to discuss during the meal. As in all cultures, try to avoid heavy topics, such as sensitive political issues or religious disputes. Our rule of thumb is: follow the host's lead and discuss whatever topics your host initiates.

Practice makes perfect...

Chopsticks are not just eating utensils

Close the Business Banquet

There is no banquet on earth that never ends. When the last dish is finished, the banquet will come to an official end. There is usually no ceremony marking the conclusion of a banquet. The host may ask if you have eaten your fill. Then the principal host will rise, signaling that the banquet has ended. Generally, the principal host will bid good evening to everyone at the door and stay behind to settle the bill with the restaurateur. Other hosts usually accompany you to your vehicles and wave goodbye until the cars have left the premises.

Some Eating Taboos

There are quite a number of taboos at a dinner table, as they are believed to bring bad luck to the people attending the meal. Some Chinese believe that eating is pretty much related to one's fortune. For example, when finishing one side of the fish, do not use the chopsticks to turn the fish to the other side. If the fish breaks when turning with the chopsticks, a boat will be sinking; this is especially true in Hong Kong, which was a fishing port in its early years. Never dig chopsticks in the rice, since this looks like the Chinese incense used to pay respects to the dead. Never say, "I'm finished." It implies that you are dead and will never have the chance to eat again. Instead you should say, "I'm full." Furthermore, the Chinese never serve seven dishes at a meal because meals held after funerals consist of seven dishes. All of these superstitions have become part of the Chinese table etiquette.

Chapter

14 Etiquette of Gift Exchange

xchanging gifts is a common practice among business partners throughout the world. But what and how to give are questions you have to think about when you are doing business in a different culture from your own. Presents are an important part of Chinese culture and giving and receiving gifts has become a type of art. One needs to give the right object to the right person at the right time and in the right place so that both parties feel happy, or at least do not feel uncomfortable. In this chapter, we give a brief introduction to gift giving and receiving in China, helping you avoid potential faux pas.

WHY GIVE A GIFT

For a long time, China was a people-based society ruled by hierarchical powers. Currying favor with people in power was often the only way for ordinary people to protect themselves, have wrongs redressed, or obtain basic rights. Giving a gift to a person in power could often buy such a favor. Over time, gift giving became a component of daily life for the Chinese, functioning as a means of showing goodwill, nurturing friendship, and gaining or repaying a favor. The Chinese refer to gifts as "lubricants" which can help keep the engine of a *guanxi* relationship going.

Like many places in the world, a gift is given when people attend a birthday party, visit a sick person, go to see relatives or good friends, attend a wedding, celebrate a traditional Chinese festival, such as Chinese New Year, return from a long domestic or foreign journey, thank an individual for a special service or kindness, express goodwill to a business partner for hospitality, and celebrate the completion of a business transaction. To the Chinese, the gift itself can tell a lot of things, for example, the relationship between the gift giver and receiver or the sort of favor expected from the receiver. There is a rule when giving and receiving a gift: the receiver should not open the gift immediately and in public. In addition, how to present a gift may possibly reveal the intention of a gift giver. Gift giving may be conducted publicly, for example, at a banquet to your business partner, or privately so as not to appear as a bribe.

Another important distinction with the Chinese gift culture is that it carries a strong obligation for reciprocity. Generally speaking, when one gives a present, he or she would first ensure the gratitude of the recipient and, second, scale and balance the advantages that he or she can gain from the recipient. The recipient will continue the balancing process and scale what should be given back. It can be another gift similar in value and fit for the occasion and the position of the recipient. It can be a favor, such as introducing a new business relationship or a local government official who is key to business operations in a particular area. Gift giving in China has therefore developed into an art. What to give, how to give, and to whom you should give may determine your business success in China.

Please kindly accept this small gift of mine!

Here we want to stress one point: the significant difference in the way Chinese and Westerners express appreciation for favors. Westerners generally express gratitude verbally with a simple "thank you," casual or emotional, depending on the situation. However, the Western "thank you" can be for trivial things in the eyes of the Chinese, for example, when someone opens a door for you, hands you a glass of water, and so on. The Chinese, on the other hand, express their appreciation in tangible forms like gifts and other favors. Simply saying "thanks" is not enough to show one's appreciation for a big favor received. Generally speaking, the Chinese believe that favors should be repaid materially, and giving and receiving should be reciprocal. They regard Westerners' frequent use of "thank you" as a glib and insincere way of passing off obligation. If all you can do or choose to do is say "thanks," it should be very specific and sincere, and then stop. The Chinese do not like gushy thanks.

Gift giving between Chinese and foreigners has been a controversial subject for the government. Before international business exchanges went into high gear in China, individuals receiving presents were ordered to turn them over to their work units to be shared by all in a spirit of equality. Nowadays, there is a law in China forbidding government officials from accepting gifts as they are considered bribery and can cause unfair competition. Regulations introduced in 2002 specified gifts worth over RMB 1,500 as bribes, especially when given in the form of cash. Many countries have laws that proscribe their citizens from giving bribes in foreign countries. So if you want to maintain a healthy business relationship with your Chinese partners, you should be very careful when giving and receiving gifts.

WHAT TO GIVE

Generally, the Chinese are reticent about what they would like to receive as gifts from relatives, friends, or newly made foreign contacts. You should prepare some gifts for a business trip to China. It is best if these gifts are business related rather than items intended for personal use. It is more appropriate to bring one large gift to the host institution and small gifts to individual members of the Chinese team. The gifts should be more memorable rather than practical. Avoid expensive and valuable items since they are more likely to suggest impropriety and smack of bribery, which may cause problems for you and the recipient. Gifts are not expected on the first visit, but they can be given if you feel that the beginning of a relationship has been established. Presenting a gift to someone on a personal basis is best done in private.

The gift could be a craft piece, an art object, or a coffee-table book. Gifts to individuals should be of lesser value, from US$10 to US$15. Any gift that is valued over RMB 500 (around US$70) will be viewed as an expensive gift by Chinese standards. The corporate gift should be presented to the head of the Chinese group at the dinner banquet or at the conclusion of a business meeting. If gifts are to be given to several individuals, make sure that each person receives a gift of roughly equal value. The gifts may be placed on the table at a dinner banquet or presented at an appropriately relaxed time. If you give many gifts, do not ignore anyone who is present or anyone who has shown hospitality during your stay. Bring along extra gifts just in case.

If you are invited to a Chinese home, it is courteous to arrive with a small gift. Suitable presents include a basket of fruit, tea, flowers, or any memento from your home country. Picture books of your hometown would make good presents. Presenting the hostess with perfume or children with toys would also be appreciated. Foreign liquor is another gift that is much appreciated. French cognac is the most prized, although it can be rather expensive and should only be given to those with whom you already have a personal relationship. Appreciated gifts can include the following:

- Branded vitamins, Western-grown ginseng, fish oil, and calcium
- Boxed chocolate and sweets
- Branded cosmetics and perfumes
- Picture books
- Fine liquor
- Books or framed paintings of your country
- Commemorative stamps, coins, or mugs
- Leather belts and cardholders
- Children's toys
- Branded coffee beans

There are some things you should never give a Chinese as a gift. Don't give a clock to an old Chinese because *"song zhong"* (literally translated as "giving a clock as a gift") sounds like "attending one's funeral" in Chinese. One should not give a pair of shoes to an older Chinese either because *"song xie"* ("giving a pair of shoes as a gift") sounds similar to "giving evil to someone." One must also guard against giving a green hat as a gift to a Chinese man as "wearing a green hat" in Chinese implies the man is cheated by his wife who is having an affair with another man. Gifts to avoid:

- Clocks
- Shoes
- Green hats
- Knives
- Scissors

How to Present a Gift

When you give a gift to your Chinese friend, you may encounter a situation that puzzles many foreigners. Your Chinese friend will decline the gift you have carefully chosen rather than happily accept it as you usually do in the West. Don't assume that your friend doesn't like your gift. This is a typical Chinese way of accepting the offering. By saying no, the Chinese believe they have displayed modesty and politeness and avoided being considered greedy by gift giver. You should insist on giving the gift until your friend finally accepts it. This back-and-forth ritual of gift rejection and coercion is quite alien to most Westerners, but keep in mind that it's like a game and the Chinese does not really intend to decline the gift. Even knowing something about this game doesn't make it easy to determine how far you have to go in repeating the offerings until the receiver accepts your gift with appropriate expressions of appreciation and gratitude. It may have to repeat three or four rounds or even more.

There will be times when someone genuinely does not want to accept your gift. The reason your gift is refused may be that he doesn't want to owe you a favor or he has no intention of starting a *guanxi*. So after your repeated attempts to give a present are rejected, you will need to withdraw your offer.

Even when the gift is finally accepted, you may still feel uncomfortable. The Chinese tend not to open a gift in front of the gift giver and other people. This doesn't mean they don't like your gift; rather, they are being modest, trying not to appear greedy, and saving the face of the giver so that the gift's value and appropriateness will not be evaluated in public. In this situation, you can suggest to your friend that he should open the gift to see what it is inside.

On formal occasions, exchanging gifts is often scheduled after the speeches of the heads of the two parties. The polite way to present and receive a gift is to use both hands outstretched. There is no refuse-accept game in this instance and both sides will immediately open the gifts and show them to the public. You should shake hands with each other after the ceremony.

Any gift that you give to the Chinese should be wrapped in the traditional lucky colors of gold or red. White and black are considered colors of mourning in Chinese culture. In terms of wrapping, Westerners like to receive beautifully wrapped gifts, even if it's just a small box of chocolates. But the Chinese generally value what is inside the wrapping more than outside, so you may receive a gift from a Chinese that is not delicately wrapped but which is of real value.

How to Receive a Gift

When a gift is offered to you, it is not necessary for you to refuse it ceremonially as the Chinese do. Humble acceptance and a few choice words of appreciation are fine. A gift from a Chinese business person may simply be a courtesy accorded to all visitors, but it can also be an acknowledgement that a relationship exists with you. Or it may indicate that you will be asked for a favor.

After you accept the gift, please do not open it in front of the giver. If you are curious about what is inside, you can ask the gift presenter if you can take a look. When you open it, don't do it in a hasty way. Tearing the wrappings off is a sign of greediness. Or you can open it when you are alone and then call to express your appreciation, write a thank you card, or thank the giver in person.

Sometimes you may receive an expensive present from a Chinese colleague. Possible motives may be that the gift-giver treasures his relationship with you or he gives it to you as some kind of social investment and expects you to reciprocate at some future date. In this situation, our advice is that you can give an expensive gift in return to your Chinese friend or business partner or you assiduously refuse any unusually expensive gifts. Otherwise, you may unwittingly become involved in an ongoing series of obligations and favor exchanges. Remember the case about the American professor in Chapter 7? Basically there is no free lunch. If you receive something expensive, you will be expected to return something of similar value or greater in the future.

Chapter

15 Counting Your Way to a Colorful Success

By this stage in the book you should feel confident about how to conduct yourself in China. In this chapter we explore the implications and associations of numbers and colors that are considered lucky, for example, those used for weddings or holiday decorations. By the same token, some numbers and colors should be avoided on certain occasions. Choosing the right date and the right color is important to your business.

NUMBERS AND THEIR IMPLICATIONS

Numbers play an important role in our daily life as well as in business. For example, we need a telephone number or a date for opening a business. Numbers in different cultures carry special meanings associated with history, tradition, and pronunciation. Some numbers in Chinese are considered positive while others are negative. For example, in the Daoist tradition, odd numbers are considered to be male or *yang* while even numbers are feminine or *yin*. People prefer to choose an even number (year, month, and day) for their wedding day. It would be best if both the lunar and Gregorian calendar happen to be even numbers. Like a lot of Chinese superstitions, a lucky number often has to do with the pronunciation of the word. Since you are doing business in China or with the Chinese, you should know some basics about numbers in the culture; otherwise you may come across pitfalls without knowing why. The implied meanings associated with the first ten numbers in Chinese are given below:

Zero, pronounced *ling*, sounds like "effective," "wonderful," "work well," and "excellent" in Chinese. People like to put zero before or after the numbers six, seven, and eight, which respectively mean "effective smoothness," "effective rising," and "effective prosperity."

One, pronounced *yi* in Chinese, sounds like "assured," "sure," "definitely," and is considered lucky when positioned in front of number eight, which means "prosperity." It is also pronounced *yao* (meaning "want") in telephone numbers. Therefore the number 18 means "want to become prosperous" or "definitely/surely be prosperous."

Two in Cantonese is pronounced *yee*, a homonym for "easy." It is good when combined with number eight meaning "easy prosperity." It also means *lai* (come) in Shanghai dialect, which means "prosperity is coming/has come." As the first even number, it suggests the balance of two, harmonious coexistence, and to some extent, birth of a new life.

Three, pronounced *san*, is close to the sound for "life," suggesting "life," "birth," or "living." It also sounds like *zai* (again) in Shanghai dialect, which contains a very positive meaning when followed by numbers six, seven, and eight. They imply respectively "doing things smoothly again," "rising again," and "become prosperous again."

Four is the unluckiest number of all for the Chinese, as well as for Japanese and Koreans. It sounds like the word "death" or "to die" in all three languages. Consequently, it is very unlucky to give gifts in a group of four. A lot of Chinese people try to avoid buying a house with the number four in the address or being assigned a telephone number with four in it. The fourth floor is usually the cheapest floor to live on and is often occupied by foreigners who don't know the connotation of the number four.

Five, pronounced *wu* in Standard Chinese or Putonghua, sounds like "I." The numbers 517, 518, 538 mean "I will rise," "I will prosper," and "I will extremely prosper."

Six is another lucky number, only second to number eight, because the pronunciation sounds like the word for "flow," suggesting that everything will go smoothly. This number is auspicious because people associate it with the meaning "successful" and "smooth." There are many set phrases that describe certain phenomena with the number six in it, for example: the six relatives closest to a person (parents and four siblings); the six roots of desire a man must purify before he can become a monk; the six inclinations; the six feelings of man; the six colors; the six classic books, and so on. A number which combines six with other lucky numbers is much sought after.

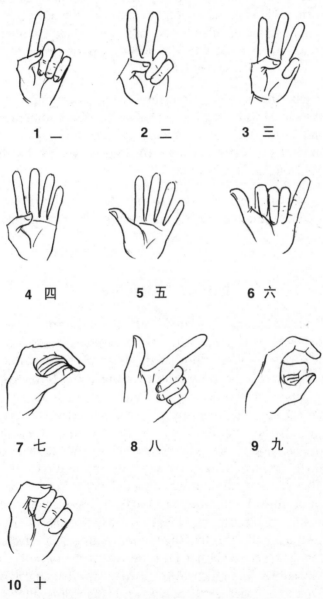

Chinese number gestures

Seven is another lucky number because it sounds like the word for "guaranteed," "rise," and "togetherness." The numbers 176 and 178 mean respectively "going smoothly together" and "getting prosperous together."

Eight, pronounced *ba,* is generally considered the luckiest number because it sounds like *fa,* meaning "to prosper" and "make a fortune" in Chinese. It can be used in combination with numbers one through nine, and all are for good fortune. House and telephone numbers containing the number eight are extremely sought after, for example, the Beijing Olympics start on 08/08/2008 at 8 p.m. The people who own the online casino 888.com certainly know why they chose that URL.

Nine sounds like the word for "a long time." It's another popular lucky number as it's associated with dragons and longevity. When combined with the number eight it means "prosper immediately." The Old People's Festival falls on September 9th every year in China. This date carries good wishes for the elders to live a long and healthy life.

Ten is not a lucky number because it sounds like four when pronounced by people from the southern part of China, including Taiwan, Hong Kong, and Macau.

Lucky Numbers

Knowing some nuances associated with numbers can help foreigners better understand why many Chinese businesses flocked to the San Gabriel Valley of Southern California: this is simply because the area code in that vicinity was 818 or "prosperity guaranteed and sure prosperity!" If you are a business person dealing with numbers, such as accounts, loan officers, real estate agents, sales people, or developers, you may want to consider seriously how numbers impact your business. Are some of your most unpopular models or resale homes not selling? Is there one numbered 1400 ("guaranteed and sure death, effective and effective")? Or do you know that you can sell a house numbered 28928 in a minute to someone who wants to fork out an extra $100,000? The reason is simple: the number means "easy prosperity, longevity, easy prosperity." In addition, with nine in the middle, this five-digit number suggests perfect balance.

When giving flowers, it's best to give one, two, three, or nine. One means that the lucky lady is your one true love, two means that all you need is for the two of you to be together, three represents the words "I love you," and nine means that your love will last forever.

An auction of auspicious car plate numbers in Shanghai

Lucky numbers are a big industry in China. A glance at business telephone numbers listed in any Chinese telephone directory will reveal how seriously the Chinese take auspicious numbers. The following is a sampling of the telephone numbers chosen by some Chinese businesses and Chinese restaurants: 8888-8888; 6688-8687; 8888-8686; 8980-8808; 8181-5858; 6666-8800; 2828-8998; 9818-3388; 2828-2288, 9818-9188, etc.

Auctioning auspicious telephone numbers or car plate numbers has become very popular in some big cities in China. The most expensive number is 8888. At a telephone number auction in Shanghai on March 21, 1992, the starting price for a telephone number with 8888 was RMB 30,000 which eventually sold for RMB 46,000.

Choosing telephone numbers is something of a game in which you can string together numbers that sound like words to form sentences.

0 – sounds like "you"
1 – sounds like "want" or "will"
2 – sounds like "love"
3 – sounds like "again," "live," or "birth"
4 – sounds like "death"
5 – sounds like "I" or "none"
6 – sounds like "smoothly"
7 – sounds like "family," "wife," or "together"
8 – sounds like "prosperity" (or "get rich")
9 – sounds like "a long time" (or "forever")

So a very romantic telephone number would end in 5257 ("I love my wife") and an up and coming businessman might choose 518 ("I will get rich"). Someone in a hurry to get married might choose 517 ("I want a wife"), but the man who chooses 51574 might not be very popular at home for a very long time.

COLORS AND THEIR IMPLICATIONS

Like numbers, colors also have meanings. When you see the following colors you may have associations with certain meanings or occasions: black and orange; red and green; black and yellow; and red, white, and blue. Your association may be: Halloween, Christmas, a bumble-bee, and an American flag. In Chinese culture, colors also have hidden meanings. If you use the wrong colored ink when printing someone's name or decorating your showroom in colors associated with death, it may bring "deadly" bad luck to your business. The following descriptions of the Chinese meaning of colors will give you a basic idea and help you avoid cross-cultural mistakes:

Red stands for joy and happiness to the Chinese. Just like "red-letter" days on calendars for celebration in the United States, Chinese clients and customers may choose a "red number day" to celebrate a birthday, move into a new house, open a business, or conduct a birthday party or a wedding ceremony. Red is the color brides wear on their wedding day and is also the color of Chinese New Year. During the holiday season, most women wear red and the house is decorated in red. Even so, the color red also represents fire, which may burn things down, so avoid using red ink in your bank or office where Asian customers have to sign their names. To some, the appearance of one's name in red ink is associated with being deceased. When a criminal is sentenced to death his name is written in red ink with a large, black ink mark across the top of it.

Purple was always associated with heaven and the emperor in China. In olden times, the imperial court forbade common people to wear purple-colored clothes. People tend not to wear purple-colored clothes to weddings as purple is known to be the quickest color to fade; wearing purple would mean that the love or marriage may suffer the same fate.

Blue is an unlucky color in China. To the Chinese, it is unlucky to wear blue flowers or ribbons in one's hair. Wearing a blue yarn flower pinned on their dresses is a sign of mourning for women. The ultramarine blue is a funeral color worn by many Chinese.

Green is a wonderful color to the Chinese, meaning health, growth, birth, family life, wood, youth, prosperity, and harmony. If you look around in your local Chinatown, you will see how popular this color is as a roofing material, table cloth, or chair color.

Yellow represents the earth for the Chinese and is another imperial color. Daoist monks wear the color gold while Buddhist monks wear orange. Yellow chrysanthemums are a funeral flower to Japanese, Chinese, and Koreans.

White is the funeral color throughout the Chinese world. The Chinese use white and yellow chrysanthemums for funeral floral sprays and wreaths. These two colors are nowhere to be seen on either business or happy personal occasions in China. However, young people nowadays like to wear white on their wedding day under the influence of the Western culture and they believe white stands for purity and innocence.

Black is associated with guilt, evil, death, and mourning. Many Chinese like the combination of black and red, but not black and white as this is a funeral combination.

In addition, women should avoid wearing red, white, blue, or black to a Chinese wedding. The first is reserved for the bride and the remaining colors are associated with mourning. When presenting gifts to your Chinese friends, neighbors, business associates, or partners, you should use pastel colors (or red for a wedding) but not white. You may also want to skip the black bows and ribbons. For the Chinese, black is an inappropriate color for gift wrapping.

The Tiffany store in Shanghai uses pink ribbon
for its diamond jewelry boxes

Appendices

Appendices

Appendix A

Timeline in Chinese History

Dates	Dynasties	Chaodai—朝代
2070 BC–1600 BC	Xia	Xia—夏
1600 BC–1046 BC	Shang	Shang—商
1046 BC–771 BC	Western Zhou	Xizhou—西周
770 BC–256 BC	Eastern Zhou	Dongzhou—东周
	770 BC–476 BC Spring and Autumn Period	Chunqiu Shidai— 春秋时代
	475 BC–256 BC Warring States Period	Zhanguo Shidai—战国时代
221 BC–206 BC	Qin	Qin—秦
206 BC–AD 25	Western Han	Xihan—西汉
25–220	Eastern Han	Donghan—东汉
220–280	Three Kingdoms	Sanguo—三国
	220–265 Wei	Wei—魏
	221–263 Shu	Shu—蜀
	222–280 Wu	Wu—吴
265–317	Western Jin	Xijin—西晋
317–420	Eastern Jin	Dongjin—东晋

(Continued)

Dates	Dynasties			Chaodai—朝代
420–589	Southern and Northern Dynasties			Nanbeichao—南北朝
		Southern Dynasties		Nanchao—南朝
	420–589		420–479 Song	Song—宋
			479–502 Qi	Qi—齐
			502–557 Liang	Liang—梁
			557–589 Chen	Chen—陈
		Northern Dynasties		Beichao—北朝
	386–581		386–534 Northern Wei	Beiwei—北魏
			534–550 Eastern Wei	Dongwei—东魏
			535–556 Western Wei	Xiwei—西魏
			550–577 Northern Qi	Beiqi—北齐
			557–581 Northern Zhou	Beizhou—北周
581–618	Sui			Sui—隋
618–907	Tang			Tang—唐
907–960	Five Dynasties			Wudai—五代
	907–923 Later Liang			Houliang—后梁
	923–936 Later Tang			Houtang—后唐
	936–947 Later Jin			Houjin—后晋
	947–950 Later Han			Houhan—后汉
	951–960 Later Zhou			Houzhou—后周
960–1279	Song			Song—宋
	960–1127 Northern Song			Beisong—北宋
	1127–1279 Southern Song			Nansong—南宋
916–1125	Liao			Liao—辽
1038–1227	Western Xia			Xixia—西夏
1115–1234	Jin			Jin—金
1206–1368	Yuan			Yuan—元
1368–1644	Ming			Ming—明
1644–1911	Qing			Qing—清
1912–1949	Republic of China			Zhonghua Minguo—中华民国
1949–present	People's Republic of China (PRC)			Zhonghua Renmin Gongheguo—中华人民共和国

Major Historical Milestones after the Founding of the PRC

B

1949   **Founding of the PRC**: On October 1, 1949, Mao Zedong proclaimed the founding of the People's Republic of China in Beijing. The new government assumed control of a people exhausted by a century of wars and chaos, and an economy devastated by high inflation and the disruption of the transportation and communications systems. Chinese leaders quickly installed a new political and economic order modeled on the Soviet example.

1958   **The Great Leap Forward**: In 1958, China broke with the Soviet model and announced a new economic program, the "Great Leap Forward," aimed at rapidly raising industrial and agricultural production. Giant cooperatives (communes) were formed, and "backyard factories" dotted the Chinese landscape. The results were disastrous. Normal market mechanisms were disrupted, agricultural production fell behind, and people all over China exhausted themselves producing what turned out to be shoddy, unsalable goods. Within a year, starvation appeared even in fertile agricultural areas. From 1960 to 1961, the combination of poor planning during the Great Leap Forward and bad weather resulted in a great famine.

1966–1976 **The Cultural Revolution** was a power struggle within the Chinese Communist Party that escalated into large-scale social, political, and economic chaos and eventually brought the entire country to the brink of civil war. In the early 1960s, President Liu Shaoqi and Party General Secretary Deng Xiaoping adopted pragmatic economic policies that were at odds with Mao Zedong's revolutionary vision. Dissatisfied with China's new direction and his own reduced authority, Mao launched a massive political attack on Liu, Deng, and other pragmatists on May 16, 1966. The ten years of turmoil ended after Mao died in 1976.

1978 The Third Plenary Session of the 11th Central Committee of the CCP was held and the Chinese leadership adopted economic reform policies known as the Four Modernizations. These policies aimed at increasing rural income, encouraging enterprise reforms, reducing central planning, and establishing foreign direct investment in China. The year marked the beginning of China's economic reforms and open-door policy.

1992 Deng Xiaoping went on a Southern Tour to re-launch his policies on economic reforms. Since then, China has continued to implement economic reforms and opened itself wider to the outside world. The government strategies for achieving that goal include privatization of loss-making state-owned enterprises, globalizing its economy, downsizing the government bureaucracy, and so on.

2001 China joined the World Trade Organization on December 11, 2001 and formalized an agreement on conditions allowing it to enter the WTO: 1) reduce China's average tariff rates from 21.2% to 17% by 2004; 2) eliminate China's non-tariff trade restrictions on wheat, rice, corn, cotton, soybean oil, sugar, and wool; 3) open China's financial service industry to foreign banks and investors by 2007. The WTO membership has further stimulated China's economic reforms and development.

Appendix C

Different Forms of Foreign Investment in China

EQUITY JOINT VENTURE (EJV)

EJV is also known as Chinese–Foreign Joint Venture (CFJV). It is established when foreign companies, enterprises, and other economic organizations or individuals and their Chinese partners invest together in China. Both parties are responsible for the profit and loss of the joint venture. Investment can come in the form of capital, buildings, industrial property, or equipment, amongst other things. In general, the level of investment from the foreign company should not be less than 25%. The EJVs are some of the first forms of China's absorption of foreign direct investment and they account for the largest portion of FDI.

CONTRACTUAL JOINT VENTURE (CJV)

CJV enterprises are also known as China–Foreign Co-operative Enterprises (CFCE) with foreign investors providing all or most of the funds, Chinese enterprises or individuals providing land, factory buildings, available apparatus and facilities—some also provide funding. The main difference from EJV is that the investment of the parties involved will not necessarily be converted into ratios of investment.

WHOLLY FOREIGN-OWNED ENTERPRISES (WFOE)

WFOEs are established by foreign companies, enterprises, other economic organizations or individuals, who provide all of the funding. WFOEs should be able to promote the development of China's national economy, and at least meet with one of the following conditions: adopting internationally advanced technology and mechanisms; most or all products exported.

JOINT DEVELOPMENT COMPANIES (JDC)

JDC status, also known as Holding Companies (HC), has recently been given to multinational corporations by China's Ministry of Foreign Trade and Economic Cooperation (MOFTEC) to establish sole foreign-invested holding companies or by businesses jointly founded with Chinese investors to engage in direct investment for the exploration and development of natural resources, such as coal, oil, and natural gas.

BUILD–OPERATE–TRANSFER (BOT)

BOT is a type of private business investment utilized by a government to build infrastructure projects, such as highways, railways, power stations, and so on. BOTs have been gradually utilized by the Chinese government to encourage foreign investment in infrastructure projects. Commitment by the government is the key point of BOT, but the commitment by the Chinese government is not easily obtained.

FOREIGN FUNDED JOINT STOCK COMPANY (JSC)

JSC refers to companies set up by foreign companies, enterprises, or individual foreign or Chinese shareholders. The foreign shareholders are allowed to hold at least 25% of the total special category B shares of approved companies listed on the Stock Exchange in China. JSC is a legal entity and treated as foreign invested enterprises.

Chinese Provinces, Regions, and Municipalities

Provinces (24)	Sheng 省	Capital Cities	Shenghui 省会
Anhui	安徽省	Hefei	合肥市
Fujian	福建省	Fuzhou	福州市
Gansu	甘肃省	Lanzhou	兰州市
Guangdong	广东省	Guangzhou	广州市
Guangxi	广西省	Nanning	南宁市
Guizhou	贵州省	Guiyang	贵阳市
Hainan	海南省	Haikou	海口市
Hebei	河北省	Shijiazhuang	石家庄市
Heilongjiang	黑龙江省	Ha'erbin	哈尔滨市
Henan	河南省	Zhengzhou	郑州市
Hubei	湖北省	Wuhan	武汉市
Hunan	湖南省	Changsha	长沙市
Jiangsu	江苏省	Nanjing	南京市
Jiangxi	江西省	Nanchang	南昌市
Jilin	吉林省	Changchun	长春市

(Continued)

Provinces (24)	Sheng 省	Capital Cities	Shenghui 省会
Liaoning	辽宁省	Shenyang	沈阳市
Qinghai	青海省	Xining	西宁市
Shandong	山东省	Jinan	济南市
Shanxi	山西省	Taiyuan	太原市
Shaanxi	陕西省	Xi'an	西安市
Sichuan	四川省	Chengdu	成都市
Taiwan	台湾省	Taibei	台北市
Yunnan	云南省	Kunming	昆明市
Zhejiang	浙江省	Hangzhou	杭州市

Municipalities*	Zhixiashi—直辖市
Beijing	北京市
Chongqing	重庆市
Shanghai	上海市
Tianjin	天津市

*These are the four largest cities in China. Although all of them are situated in provinces they are separate entities known in Chinese as *Zhixiashi*, operating directly under the central government.

Autonomous Regions	Zizhiqu 自治区	Capital Cities	Shenghui 省会
Guangxi Zhuang Autonomous Region	广西壮族自治区	Nanning	南宁市
Inner Mongolia Autonomous Region	内蒙古自治区	Huhehot	呼和浩特市
Ningxia Hui Autonomous Region	宁夏回族自治区	Yinchuan	银川市
Tibet Autonomous Region	西藏自治区	Lhasa	拉萨市
Xinjiang Uighur Autonomous Region	新疆维吾尔自治区	Urumchi	乌鲁木齐市

Special Administrative Regions (SAR)	Tebie Xingzheng Qu 特别行政区
Macao Special Administrative Region	澳门特别行政区
Hong Kong Special Administrative Region	香港特别行政区

Structure of the Chinese Government

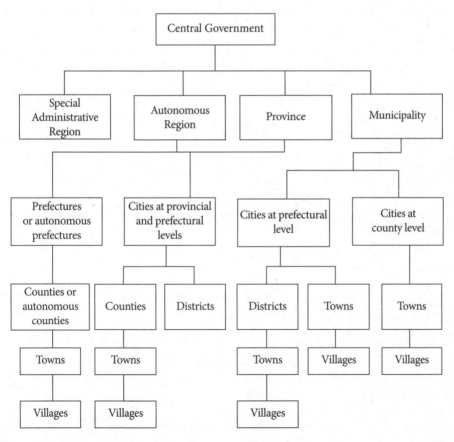

Organization of the Chinese Government

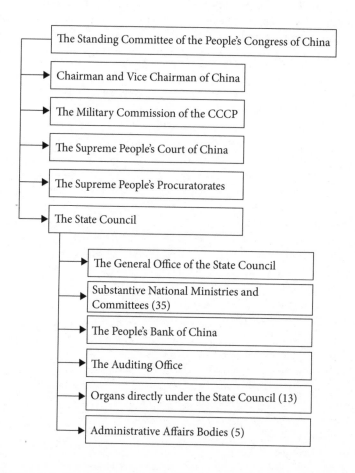

The Standing Committee of the People's Congress of China

Chairman and Vice Chairman of China

The Military Commission of the CCCP

The Supreme People's Court of China

The Supreme People's Procuratorates

The State Council

The General Office of the State Council

Substantive National Ministries and Committees (35)

The People's Bank of China

The Auditing Office

Organs directly under the State Council (13)

Administrative Affairs Bodies (5)

THE CHINESE GOVERNMENT

The Chinese Government has always been subordinate to the CCP; its role is to implement party policies. The primary organs of state power are the National People's Congress (NPC), the President, and the State Council. Members of the State Council include the premier, a variable number of vice premiers, five state councilors (protocol equal of vice premiers but with narrower portfolios), and 29 ministers and heads of State Council Commissions. Under the Chinese Constitution, the NPC is the highest organ of state power in China. It meets annually for about two weeks to review and approve major new policy directions, laws, the budget, and major personnel changes. These initiatives are presented to the NPC for consideration by the State Council after previous endorsement by the Communist Party's Central Committee. Although the NPC generally approves State Council policy and personnel recommendations, various NPC committees hold active debate in closed sessions and changes may be made to accommodate alternate views. When the NPC is not in session, its permanent organ, the Standing Committee, exercises state power.

G | Chinese Holidays

In China, the traditional calendar is known as the Agricultural Calendar (*Nongli*) while the Gregorian calendar is known as the Common Calendar (*Gongli*). Another name for the traditional Chinese calendar is the *Yin* Calendar (*Yinli*), implying the lunar aspect of the calendar, whereas the Gregorian calendar is the *Yang* Calendar (*Yangli*) referring to its solar properties. All Chinese traditional holidays are celebrated as per the lunar calendar. Therefore, the first day of the first month does not necessarily mean January 1st.

National holidays in China fall into two types: those enjoyed by all citizens and those enjoyed only by some citizens. New Year's Day, Spring Festival (Chinese New Year), *Qingming* Festival, May Day, Dragon Boat Festival, Mid-autumn Festival, and National Day are celebrated by all Chinese citizens. Among these are two Golden Weeks that fall in May and October respectively. Both holidays last for three days, but by combining two weekends with them, people actually enjoy seven consecutive days off. During these two weeks, most people go shopping or holidaying, forming a strong boost to China's economy.

Chinese holidays Traditional/ non-Traditional	Date	Length of holiday
New Year's Day	January 1	1 day
Spring Festival	1st day of the 1st lunar month	3 days (New Year's Eve, 1st and 2nd day of the first lunar month)
Lantern Festival	15th of the 1st lunar month	No days off
International Women's Day	March 8	Half day for women
Tree-Planting Day	April 1	No days off
Qingming (Clear and Bright) Festival	April 4 or 5	1 day
May Day	May 1	1 day
Youth Day	May 4	Half day for the youth over 14 years old
International Nurses' Day	May 12	No days off
Children's Day	June 1	1 day for children under 14 years old
Dragon Boat Festival	5th day of the 5th lunar month	1 day
Birthday of the Chinese Communist Party	July 1	No days off
Army's Day	August 1	Half day for active army
Teachers' Day	September 10	No days off
Mid-Autumn Festival	15th day of the 8th lunar month	1 day
National Day	October 1	3 days (October 1st, 2nd and 3rd)
Journalist Day	November 8	No days off

Typical Dishes of Local Chinese Cuisines

H

Anhui Cuisine

English	Chinese
Huangshan Braised Pigeon	*Huangshan zhengge*
Hot Diced Pork	*shijin rouding*
Wuwei Smoked Duck	*Wuwei xunya*

Beijing Cuisine

English	Chinese
Beijing Roast Duck	*Beijing kaoya*
Instant-boiled Mutton Mongolian Hot Pot	*shuan yangrou*
Braised Shark's Fin	*huangmen yuchi*
Sautéed Chicken With Green Peppers	*jiangbao jiding*
Sweet Cake With Dates	*saqima*

Fujian Cuisine

English	Chinese
Buddha Jumps Over the Wall	*fo tiaoqiang*
Snow Chicken	*xuehua ji*
Prawn with Dragon's Body and Phoenix's Tail	*fengwei xia*

Guangdong Cuisine

English	Chinese
Shark's Fin Soup	*yuchi tang*
Steamed Sea Bass	*qingzheng luyu*
Roast Suckling pig	*kao ruzhu*
Iron Plate Beef	*tieban niurou*
Sweet and Sour Pork	*gulao rou*

Hunan Cuisine

English	Chinese
Dong'an Chick	*dong'an ziji*
Peppery and Hot Chick	*mala ziji*
Lotus Seedpods with Rock Sugar	*bingtang xianglian*

Jiangsu Cuisine

English	Chinese
Stewed Crab with Clear Soup	*qingzheng xie*
Long-boiled and Dry-shredded Meat	*qingdun xiefen shizitou*
Crystal Meat	*shuijing yaoti*
Jinling Salted Dried Duck	*jinling yanshui ya*

Shandong Cuisine

English	Chinese
Trumpet Shell Braised in Soy Sauce	*hongshao hailuo*
Sweet and Sour Carp	*tangcu liyu*
Dezhou Stewed Chicken	*dezhou paji*
Caramelized Apple	*basi pingguo*

Shanghai Cuisine

English	Chinese
Sour and Hot Soup with Eel and Chicken	*longfeng suanla tang*
Black Sea Cucumber with Shrimp Roe	*xiazi dawushen*
Duck with Prawn Rounds	*ruyi ya juan xian*
Shrimps of Two Colors	*shuangse xiaren*
Boiled Crucian Carp with Clam	*geli cuan jiyu*
Steamed Beef in Rice Flour	*yuanlong fenzheng niurou*

Sichuan Cuisine

English	Chinese
Sliced Cold Chicken	*xiao jianji*
Twice Cooked Pork	*hui guo rou*
Shredded Pork and Hot Sauce	*yuxiang rousi*
Spicy Hot Bean Curd	*mapo doufu*
Fish Flavored Eggplant	*yuxiang qiezi*
Reflecting Beef	*dengying niurou*
Couple's Beef Fillet	*fuqi feipian*

Zhejiang Cuisine

English	Chinese
Sour West Lake Fish	*xihu cuyu*
Longjing Shelled Shrimp	*longjing xiaren*
Beggar's Chicken	*jiaohua ji*

Survival Phrases and
Sentences in Chinese

1. How do you do? / Hello. Hi. Nǐ hǎo! Ni hǎo! 你好！
2. How are you? Nǐ hǎo ma? 你好吗？
3. I am fine. Wǒ hěn hǎo. 我很好。
4. Thank you. Xièxie. 谢谢。
5. You are welcome. Bú kèqi. 不客气。
6. Goodbye. Zàijiàn. 再见。
7. What is your name? Nín jiào shénme míngzi? 您叫什么名字？
8. My name is … Wǒ jiào …… 我叫……
9. Where are you from? Nǐ shì nǎguó rén? 你是哪国人？
10. I am from America. Wǒ shì Měiguórén. 我是美国人。
11. All right. Hǎo (ba). 好（吧）。
12. No, not all right. Bù hǎo. 不好。
13. Do you speak English? Nín huì shuō Yīngyǔ ma? 您会说英语吗？
    I do. Wǒ huì; 对，我会。
    Wǒ bú huì. 不，我不会。
14. I don't. Do you speak Chinese? Ní huì shuō Hànyǔ/Zhōngwén ma? 你会说
    汉语/中文吗？
15. I don't understand. Wǒ bù dǒng. 我不懂。
16. I don't know. Wǒ bù zhīdào. 我不知道。
17. What is this called? Zhège jiào shénme? 这个叫什么？
18. I am sorry. Duìbuqǐ. 对不起。

19. No problem. Méi guānxi. 没关系。

20. Miss/waitress Xiǎojie 小姐。

21. Mister, waiter. Xiānsheng 先生。

22. Glad to meet you. Jiàn dào nǐ hěn gāoxìng. 见到你很高兴。

23. Good morning. Zǎoshàng hǎo. 早上好。

24. Good afternoon. Xiàwu hao. 下午好。

25. Good evening. Wǎnshàng hǎo. 晚上好。

26. Good luck. Zhù nǐ hǎo yùn. 祝你好运。

27. Good night. Wǎn'ān. 晚安。

28. Hope to see you again next time. Xīwàng xià cì zài jiàn dào nǐ. 希望下次再见到你。

29. How do you say … in Chinese? …… (an English word or phrase) de Zhōngwén zěnme shuō? ……的中文怎么说？

30. How is your dad and mom? Nǐ de bàba māma hǎo ma? 你的爸爸妈妈好吗？

31. How old are you? Nǐ duō dà? 你多大？

32. I am John. Wǒ shì Yuēhàn. 我是约翰。

33. I don't speak English. Wǒ bú huì shuō Yīngyǔ / Yīngwén. 我不会说英语/英文。

34. Let me introduce you to each other. Wǒ gěi nǐmen jièshào yí xiàr. 我给你们介绍一下儿。

35. May I speak with (name of person)? Wǒ kěyǐ hé (name of person) shuōhuà ma? 我可以和 …… 说话吗？

36. My first name is John and my last name is Smith. Wǒ jiào Yuēhàn, wǒxing Shǐmìsī. 我叫约翰，我姓史密斯。

37. Say hi to Mrs. Li. Dài wèn Lǐ Tàitai hǎo. 代问李太太好。

38. See you tomorrow! Míngtiān jiàn. 明天见。

39. So-so. Mǎ mǎ hū hū. 马马虎虎。

40. Please speak slowly. Qǐng shuō màn diǎnr. 请说慢点儿。

41. That is Mr Chen. Nà wèi shì Chén Xiānsheng. 那位是陈先生。

42. Welcome to my home. Huānyíng dào wǒ jiā zuò kè. 欢迎到我家做客。

43. Bon voyage! Wish you a happy journey. Zhù nǐ lǚtú yúkuài! 祝你旅途愉快！

44. May I ask, how much is this? Qǐngwèn, zhè ge duōshao qián? 请问，这个多少钱？

45. It is too expensive. Can you sell it at a cheaper price? Tài guì le. Néng bu néng piányi diǎn? 太贵了。能不能便宜点儿？

46. Excuse me, may where is the restroom? Láojià, qǐngwèn cèsuǒ zài nǎr? 劳驾，请问，厕所在哪儿？

47. Numbers: 0 líng 零; 1 yī 一; 2 èr 二; 3 sān 三; 4 sì 四; 5 wǔ 五; 6 liù 六; 7 qī 七; 8 bā 八; 9 jiǔ 九; 10 shí 十

Select Bibliography

Ambler, T. and M. Witzel. *Doing Business in China*. London and New York: Routledge, 2004.

Axtell, R. *Gestures: The Do's and Taboos of Body Language around the World*. New York: John Wiley & Sons, 1991.

Berliner, N. *Yin Yu Tang—The Architecture and Daily Life of a Chinese House*. North Clarendon, VT: Tuttle Publishing, 2003.

Buckley, P. J., J. Clegg, and H. Tan. "Cultural Awareness in Knowledge Transfer to China—The Role of *Guanxi* and *Mianzi*." *Journal of World Business* 41, no. 3, (September 1, 2006): 275–288.

Bucknall, K. B. *Chinese Business Etiquette and Culture*. Boston: Boston Books, 1999.

Chan, A. K. K., L. Denton, and A. S. L. Tsang. "The Art of Gift Giving in China." *Business Horizons* 46, no. 4, (July 2003): 47–53.

Chan, J. L. *China Streetsmart—What You Must Know to be Effective and Profitable in China*. Singapore: Prentice Hall, 2003.

Chen, M. J. *Inside Chinese Business—A Guide for Managers Worldwide*. Boston: Harvard Business School Press, 2001.

Chen, Xiao-Ping and Chen Chao C. "On the Intricacies of the Chinese *Guanxi*: A Process Model of *Guanxi* Development." *Asia Pacific Journal of Management* 21, (September 3, 2004): 305–324.

Child, P. N. "Lessons from a Global Retailer: Interview with the President of Carrefour China." *Mckinsey Quarterly 2006 Special Edition: Serving the New Chinese Consumer*.

Ching, F. ed. *China in Transition*. Hong Kong: Review Publishing Co., 1994.

Chu, C. N. *The Asian Mind Game*. New York, Rawson Associates: McMillan Publishing Company, 1990.

De Mente, B. *Chinese Etiquette and Ethics in Business*. Lincolnwood, Illinois: NTC Business Books, 1989.

Dollar, D. "Capitalism, Globalization and Poverty." Consignment research paper written for *The Foundation for Teaching Economics*, 2003.

Engholm, C. *Doing Business in Asia's Booming "China Triangle."* Englewood Cliffs, New Jersey: Prentice Hall, 1994.

Fang, T. *Chinese Business Negotiation Style*. Thousand Oaks, California: Sage Publications Inc., 1999.

Gao, Ge and Ting-Toomey Stella. *Communicating Effectively with the Chinese*. Thousand Oaks, California: SAGE Publications Inc., 1998.

Genzberger, C. A., ed. *China Business: The Portable Encyclopedia for Doing Business with China*. San Rafael, California: World Trade Press, 1995.

Ghauri, P. N. and Tony Fang. "Negotiating with the Chinese: A Socio-Cultural Analysis." *Journal of World Business* 36, no. 3, (Autumn 2001): 303–325.

Goffman, Erving. "On Face-Work: An Analysis of Ritual Elements in Social Interaction." *Psychiatry: Journal for the Study of Interpersonal Processes* 18, no. 3, (August 1955): 213–231.

Gramham, J. L. and N. M. Lam. "The Chinese Negotiation." *Harvard Business Review* 81, no. 10, (October 2003): 82–91.

Hammond, Scott. C. and Lowell M. Glenn. "The Ancient Practice of Chinese Social Networking: *Guanxi* and Social Network Theory." *E: CO* (Special Double Issue) 6, Nos. 1–2, (2004): 24–31.

Hofstede, Geert and M. H. Bond. "The Confucius Connection: From Cultural Roots to Economic Growth." *Organizational Dynamics* 16, no. 4, (Spring 1988): 5–21.

Hu, Hsien Chin. "The Chinese concept of 'face'." *American Anthropologist* 46, no. 1, (January–March 1994): 45–64.

Hu, Wenzhong and Cornelius L. Grove. *Encountering the Chinese—A Guide for Americans*. Yarmouth, Maine: Intercultural Press, 1998.

Huang, Philip C. C. *Civil Justice in China: Representation and Practice in the Qing*. Stanford: Stanford University Press, 1996.

Huang, Quanyu, Richard S. Andrulis, and Tong Chen. *A Guide to Successful Business Relations with the Chinese—Opening the Great Wall's Gate*. New York: Routledge, 1994.

Huang, Quanyu, Joseph Leonard, and Tong Chen. *Business Decision Making in China*. New York: Routledge, 1997.

Hwang, K. K. "Face and Favor: The Chinese Power Game." *American Journal of Sociology* 92, no. 4, (1997): 944–974.

James, David L. *The Executive Guide to Asian-Pacific Communications*. New York: Kodansha America, 1995.

Lepport, Paul A. *How to Do Business with Chinese—A Taiwan Handbook for Executives*. Grawn, Michigan: Patton Pacific Press, 1984.

Lee, Charles. *Cowboys and Dragons—Shattering Cultural Myths to Advance Chinese—American Business*. Chicago: Dearborn Trade Publishing, 2003.

Lee, D. Y. and P. L. Dawes. "*Guanxi*, Trust, and Long-Term Orientation in Chinese Business Market." *Journal of International Marketing* 13, no. 2, (2005): 28–56.

Lee, Edward Yiu-chung and Alistair Anderson. "Role of *Guanxi* in Chinese Entrepreneurship." *The Journal of* Asia Entrepreneurship and Sustainability. (December 2007): 38–51.

Levine, Tyrrell and Kim Woodard. "The New Face of Chinese M&A." *Far Eastern Economic Review* 169, no. 3, (2006): 20.

Li, Xiangling. *Chinese–Dutch Business Negotiations—Insights from Discourse.* Utrecht Studies in Language and Communication 14. Amsterdam: Rodopi, 1999.

Lin, Justin Yifu, Fang Cai, and Zhou Li. "The Lessons of China's Transition to a Market Economy." *The CATO JOURNAL* 16, no. 2, (Fall 1996 edition): 201–231.

Lin, Justin Yifu, Fang Cai, and Zhou Li. *State-Owned Enterprise Reform in China.* Hong Kong: The Chinese University Press, 2001.

Liu, Meiru. *Basic Business Chinese.* Beijing: Peking University Press, 2006.

Lü, Shuxiang. *Modern Chinese Dictionary (Xiandai Hanyu Cidian).* Beijing: Commercial Press, 2005.

Ma, Debin. "Law, Commerce and Knowledge in 18–20th Century China: An Institutional Perspective on the 'Great Divergence'." *Journal of Legal Studies* 33, (June 2004): 475–515.

Ma, Debin. "Law and Commerce in Traditional China, an Institutional Perspective on the 'Great Divergence'." *Keizai-Shirin* 73, no. 4, (March 2006): 69–96.

McClenahen, J. S. "China's Cultural Challenge." *Industry Week* 253, no. 4, (2004): 38–45.

McGregor, J. *One Billion Customers,* 1st edition. New York: Free Press, 2005.

Pye, Lucian W. *Chinese Negotiation Style—Commercial Approaches and Cultural Principles.* Westport: Quorum Books, 1992.

Qian, Yingyi. "The Process of China's Market Transition (1978–98): The Evolutionary, Historical, and Comparative Perspectives." *Journal of Institutional and Theoretical Economics* 156, no. 1, (March 2000): 151–171.

Redding, S. G. and M. Ng. "The Role of 'Face' in the Organizational Perceptions of Chinese Managers." *Organization Studies* 3, no. 3, (1982): 201–210.

"Reform of China's State-owned Enterprises." In *Beyond Transition–The Newsletter about Reforming Economies.* A Progress Report of Oxford Analytica. *Asia Pacific Daily Briefs of Oxford Analytica.* 2001.

Saxon, M. *An American's Guide to Doing Business in China,* 1st edition. Avon, Massachusetts: Adams Media, an F+W Publications Company, 2007.

Seligman, Scott D. *Dealing with the Chinese.* New York: Warner Books, 1989.

Sheff, D. *China Dawn.* New York: Harper Collins Publishers Inc., 2002.

Shi, X. and P. C. Wright. "The Potential Impacts of National Feelings on International Business Negotiations: A Study in the China Context." *International Business Review* 12, no. 3, (2003): 311–329.

Shirk, Susan L. *The Political Logic of Economic Reform in China.* Berkeley: University of California Press, 1993.

Sinclair, Kevin and Iris Po-yee Wong. *Culture Shock!—A Guide to Customs and Etiquette.* Portland: Graphic Arts Center Publishing Company, 2004.

Stuttard, John B. *The New Silk Road—Secrets of Business Success in China Today.* New York: John Wiley & Sons, Inc., 2000.

Vanhonacker, W. R. "*Guanxi* Networks in China." *The China business Review 31, (May–June 2004):* 48–53.

Wang, Margaret Mary. *Turning Bricks into Jade: Critical Incidents for Mutual Understanding among Chinese and Americans.* Boston: Intercultural Press, 2000.

Wong, Y. Y., Maher, T. E., and Lee, G. "The Strategy of an Ancient Warrior: An Inspiration for International Managers." *Multinational Business Review 6,* no.1, (1998): 83–93.

Wu, Jinglian. *Understanding and Interpreting Chinese Economic Reform.* Mason, Ohio: Thomson South-Western, 2005.

Yan, J. and R. Sorenson. "The Effect of Confucian Values on Succession in Family Business." *Family Business Review 19,* no. 3, (2006): 235–251.

Yeh, R. S. and J. J. Lawrence. "Individualism and Confucian Dynamism: A Note on Hofstede's Cultural Root to Economic Growth." *Journal of International Business Studies 26,* no. 3, (1995): 655–669.

Yang, M. M. H. *Gifts, Favors, and Banquets: The Art of Social Relationships in China.* Ithaca: Cornell University Press, 1994.

Zhao, Jensen J. "The Chinese Approach to International Business Negotiation." *Journal of Business Communication 37,* no. 3, (2000): 209–236.

Zinzius, Birgit. *Doing Business in the New China—A Handbook and Guide.* Westport, Connecticut: Praeger Publishers, 2004.

ONLINE RESOURCES

Balfour, F. "You Say *Guanxi,* I Say Schmoozing—How East is Meeting West and Building a Lingua Franca of Business Connections." *Business Week* (November 19,2007). http://www.businessweek.com/magazine/content/07_47/b4059066. htm? chan=search (accessed April 24, 2008).

Chan, Alvin M. "The Chinese Concepts of *Guanxi, Mianzi, Renqing* and *Bao*: Their Interrelationships and Implications for International Business." Paper submitted to the conference on *Advancing Theory, Maintaining Relevance* hosted by the School of Advertising, Marketing and Public Relations, Faculty of Business at University of Western Sydney, Brisbane Queensland, December 4–6, 2006. http://smib.vuw.ac.nz:8081/WWW/ANZMAC2006/documents/ Chan_Alvin.pdf (accessed March 16, 2008).

China GDP Growth: 1952–2007. http://www.chinability.com/GDP.htm (accessed March 25, 2007).

China's Political System. http://afe.easia.columbia.edu/china/gov/backgrnd.htm#PRC (accessed November 30, 2008).

Chinese Business Banquet. http://www.chinasuccessstories.com/2008/01/22/ chinese-business-banquet (accessed March 11, 2008).

Chinese Food: Eight Cuisine Branches. http://www.chinahand.net/products-en-132/eight-cuisine-branches.htm (accessed March 8, 2008).

Chinese Holidays & Festivals. http://www.index-china.com/index-english/chinese_holidays.htm (accessed March 28, 2008).

Doing Business with China in the Twenty-First Century – A Critical Appraisal of the Strategic Issues Encountered by Some Global Corporations. http://library.uws.edu.au/adt-NUWS/uploads/approved/adt-NUWS20040419.142707/public/04Thesis3.pdf (accessed March 22, 2008).

Foreign Investment in China. http://www.uschina.org/info/analysis/2007/june-foreign-investment.html (accessed March 12, 2008).

Fung, Kwok Chiu, Lawrence J. Lau, and Joseph, S. Lee. *U.S. Direct Investment in China*. Washington D.C.: The AEI Press, 2004, 24–27. http://www.chinahand.net/products-en-132/eight-cuisine-branches.htm (accessed January 25, 2008).

"Lessons from a global retailer: An interview with the president of Carrefour China." *The McKinsey Quarterly*. http://www.mckinseyquarterly.com/Lessons_from_a_global_retailer_An_interview_with_the_president_of_Carrefour_China (accessed March 22, 2008).

Li, Weisen. Teaching Notes. "Chinese Culture and Customs" in Lipman, Jonathan, "Chifan le meiyou?"/Have you eaten yet?" http://www.mtholyoke.edu/courses/jlipman/chifanlemeiyou.htm (accessed March 22, 2008).

Noriko Kagawa. "The Modern Enterprise System and Corporate Governance in China's State-Owned Enterprise Reform." http://www.gwu.edu/~econ270/Noriko.htm (accessed March 22, 2008).

Norton, Patrick M. and Howard Chao (2003) "Mergers and Acquisitions in China." *Topics in Chinese Law*. April edition. http://www.omm.com/web-code/webdata/ content/publications/Topics_2003_04.PDF (accessed March 22, 2008).

People's Daily. Quoted in Xin Meng, "Recent Development in China's Labor Market" published online by Asia Pacific Press (June 23, 1998). http://zenz.org/adrian/resources/labourmarket_stats.pdf (accessed March 22, 2008).

Rawski, Thomas G. "Is China's State Enterprise Problem Still Important?" prepared for a workshop on "China's SOE Reform and Privatization" at University of Tokyo (June 25, 2000). http://www.pitt.edu/~tgrawski/papers2000/SKETCH.HTM (accessed March 22, 2008).

Sina Corporation, 1998. The Chinese *Mianzi* Survey (in Chinese), 1998. http://survey.sina.com.cn/cgi-bin/polling/voterresult.cgi?viv=1988 (accessed March 16, 2008).

"State-owned Enterprises: 'Sick Patients' Waiting for a Cure?" Knowledge@Wharton, (June 19, 2003). http://knowledge.wharton.upenn.edu/article.cfm?articleid=805 (accessed March 22, 2008).

The Library of Congress Country Studies; CIA World Factbook. http://www.photius.com/countries/china/economy/china_economy_organization.html (accessed March 22, 2008).

Wen, Guanzhong James and Dianqing Xu. "The Reformability of China's State Sector." 1997. http://books.google.com/books (accessed March 22, 2008).

Resources In Chinese

Han, Zhengshun. "Guoren xingge de diyu chayi jiqi shangye wenhua biaozheng (Regional differences of China's national character and their reflection in business culture)." *Shangye shi dai (Business Times)*, 2004.

He, Qinglian. *Xiandaihua de xianjing (Traps of Modernization)*. Jinri zhongguo chubanshe (China Today Press), 1998.

Ning, Yi, ed. *Zhongguo shang dao (Chinese Way of Business)*. Zhongguo dizhen chubanshe (China Seismology Press), 2007.

Wang, Jing, ed. *Zhongguo ge sheng shangren xingge jiemi (Decode the Characters of Business People from Different Provinces)*. Zhongguo jingji chubanshe (China Economics Press), 2007.

Wang, Shuqing. "Yao bushang chengshi shangye wenhua zhe yi ke (We must make up for the missed lesson of urban business culture)." *Weihai ribao (Weihai Daily)*, (March 26, 2004).

INDEX